RUNNING AWAY
FROM HOME

To Donna —
Thankyou for your Support
and friendship — !

Stacy

RUNNING AWAY FROM HOME

TRACY A. BURGER

NEW DEGREE PRESS

COPYRIGHT © 2022 TRACY A. BURGER

RUNNING AWAY FROM HOME

ISBN   979-8-88504-641-1   *Paperback*

          979-8-88504-959-7   *Kindle Ebook*

          979-8-88504-846-0   *Ebook*

To my sisters.
Iguana made me do it.

CONTENTS

———

AUTHOR'S NOTE

—

"Toni Morrison said, 'The function of freedom is to free someone else,' and if you are no longer wracked or in bondage to a person or a way of life, tell your story. Risk freeing someone else."
—ANNE LAMOTT, *BIRD BY BIRD*

I hurry, almost run, to my car as the tears come. I fiercely force air out of my nose, attempting to expel the acrid cigarette smoke adhered there for the past four years. As I slam the door behind me, I scream—audibly, loudly—not able to stop the sour tears. My heart aches with a confusing mix of anger, sadness, frustration, rejection, sorrow, and regret. Sobbing, my head lowers to the steering wheel. I had just come from visiting my mother.

Why does she make me so crazy? Why do I *let* her make me so crazy? Am I just trying to control her? No one's ever been able to do that, that's for sure. What makes a person hold fast to misery, disease, and righteousness, while closing herself off from help, support, and love?

It had been nearly five years since Dad died and Mom moved down to Florida to live near me due to her health issues. If I'd had a better perspective, I might have recognized the writing on the wall, the futility in trying to get her to change, grow up, take care of herself, stop smoking. Maybe if I had understood the inevitable trajectory of her life, I would have been able to show more compassion and love and deepen our relationship. Instead, I continued to stand at arm's length, avoiding the dangerous chasm enveloping us for as long as I can remember. I didn't want to be any part of the woman my mother was. I was ashamed of that.

Growing up in the seventies, I saw the perfect home, exemplified on afternoon TV reruns of *Leave It to Beaver* and *The Brady Bunch,* and in weekly evening installments of *Happy Days.* June Cleaver, Carol Brady, and Marion Cunningham demonstrated mothers were a supportive, stable presence in the household, empathizing with their children and providing the required safety net for their experiences and needs. This is how I grew up, believing families were supposed to operate this way. Parents knew what they were doing and provided the perfect atmosphere in which to raise well-adjusted children, who could then continue the perfect rearing of more well-adjusted children and so on. But this is just a fallacy; a societal lie of Kool-Aid cocktail I hungrily ingested.

No one I know speaks of their mothers harshly or critically. Yes, I have seen eyes roll as friends talk about their mothers' idiosyncrasies and the sadness when reminiscing about their mothers' lives and struggles. But I can't remember anyone speaking poorly or unfavorably about their mother and their relationship. I recall a few occasions confiding in friends of how difficult my mother was, but afterward I just felt guilty. This fueled the internal shame of it being somehow my fault we didn't get along or I couldn't let her snide, contemptuous remarks roll off my back with ease.

A parent's failure to validate or respond enough to a child's emotional needs is called childhood emotional neglect (CEN) (Webb, 2014). It doesn't happen *to* a child but fails to happen *for* a child, sending the message feelings are not important or welcome. CEN isn't from one specific traumatic event. It occurs daily and silently, and it's often unnoticed until adulthood when the desire to run away and feelings of inferiority, emotional numbness, and depression become overwhelming. Blind to the realization, I learned the hard way that going through the motions is not okay. Feeling unfulfilled is not okay, and low-grade daily depression is not okay and not the way I was meant to live. I had lived most of my life exhibiting dysfunctional symptoms of CEN—being emotionally numb, questioning the meaning of life, attempting to need no one, living with depression, having difficulty discerning my own talents, and experiencing feelings of not fitting in wherever I went. Understanding this has been liberating for me and showed me a path out of my suffering.

As I learned about CEN, I also examined the shared experiences of mother-daughter relationships, the mother complex, the divine feminine, the wounded mother, and more. I don't blame my parents for how they raised my sisters and me, but I have a new understanding of their own limitations in expressing their feelings and supporting us while we developed our emotional safe ground. Children's relationships with their mothers are complicated and aren't always ideal. I've learned I am not alone in my feelings and experiences. I commiserate with Michele Rogers, who wrote in her 2010 master's thesis when her alcoholic, emotionally distant mother moved close to her, she collapsed:

*"I was trapped in a complex, a wound, addicted to self-denial
and unable to differentiate where it hurt because I believed
that I had created the perfect home life and that I was doing
everything right. I was overdoing and making sure everything
in my home life was calm and that everyone's needs were taken
care of; there was no room for shadow to be exposed because
I did not know I had a shadow, or what I was projecting that
kept me a bonded woman. I was starting to get tired, I was
sad for no apparent reason that I could put my finger on, but
having my dependent, alcoholic mother move into my safety
space was the straw that broke the camel's back ... my outer
life showed no wounds but in my inner world I felt like a
wounded bird with a broken wing—no matter how much I
adapted there were areas in my adult life where I just could
not get off the ground to fly."*

My own mother moving into my world after decades of living
twelve hundred miles apart overwhelmed and altered my
life, ultimately metamorphosing it for the better. Apparently,
the Universe knew just what I needed to reverse my unac-
knowledged downward spiral and turn me toward the light
of self-awareness and peace.

Looking back to the past and analyzing familial relationships has been empowering and insightful for me. While I
certainly haven't found the solutions to all my life's difficulties, digging into my past and taking a deeper look into the
circumstances around me and my parents as I grew up has
been incredibly humbling and enlightening. Understanding what CEN is and how it can be challenged as an adult
has aided me in that self-discovery, allowing me to process
the relationship with my parents, specifically my mother, in
ways I never did before. This led to great discussions with

my husband and sisters and has definitely deepened, and in some ways healed, components of those relationships.

I sometimes wish I had another chance at a healthy relationship with my mother—another chance at being the perfect daughter and the compassionate and patient caregiver, the model of how to navigate the last years of a dying parent. And, of course, there's the guilt—does an ex-Catholic ever get a reprieve from the guilt? The guilt about feeling so relieved those years are behind me. The guilt about forgetting how I treated her, my immaturity in dealing with her, disappointing myself, and just moving on. Over the years, I've learned I can't let my ruminating self replay my past repeatedly—that I can't go back and change the way she treated me. I can't change the hurtful things others have said to me, or my numerous mistakes, no matter how much I try to change and fix them in my mind. Replaying them only embeds them in my mind further, making it harder and harder to move past them. This book is not about that. It's about healing wounds only time, experience, maturity, and life can afford. It's about understanding where other people come from. It's about forgiveness.

This book is for lovers of memoir and true stories, people who struggle or have struggled in a rocky relationship with their mother and anyone seeking to understand personal battles with depression, dysfunctional relationships and/or inferiority complex.

THE GREEN HOUSE

"The single hardest burden for a human being to carry is the lack of nurturance in childhood."

—STEPHEN C. HAYES, *A LIBERATED MIND*

Over and over, I'd sing "Daisy Bell" while swinging, dark pig tails flopping back and forth, on the rusty swing set to the side yard of The Green House, between the old barn and the wire fence and the gravel road below. This was bliss for my five-year-old self—feeling the wind on my face, floating weightless, by myself, not a care in the world. In winter, I'd even try to dig the swing seat out of a four-foot snowdrift. I wanted to fly so badly—fly out of the numbness around me, the weight of the unspoken nothingness inside the house. I was free on that swing seat with my oversized cotton under-wear scrunched together beneath my home-sewn dress. Free of the pressure to fit in, be small, and become invisible when I went inside.

The Green House years were some of the best years of my life—maybe because I can only remember pieces of it or was just too young to fathom the dysfunction all around me.

Or maybe as young children—born expecting connection, community, and love—we only know what we have around us. We see our mothers and fathers perfect as they are until our reflection in the mirror tells us they're not.

My four sisters and I average sixteen months apart in age. My mother claimed amnesia ("How am I supposed to remember such things?") when asked in later years about the early days with five girls under age six running and toddling around screaming, pulling hair—pulling knots out of hair—wanting to eat, nurse, color, help Mommy, and get a fresh diaper change. I can only imagine the brain freeze. Dad took his coffee thermos and black metal lunch box to his nine-to-five or third-shift job at John Deere Tractor Works with regularity—five days a week, fifty weeks a year—gone by 7:00 a.m., back by 4:30 p.m. "Daddy's home! Daddy's home!" we'd shriek, jumping on the sagging cushions of the living room sofa and chair when we spotted the gold Chevy station wagon turning up the driveway.

Married for nine years when we moved to The Green House, Mom and Dad had the routine of marriage, work, and child-rearing well established. But The Green House encompassed a much larger property than they ever had. They planted and tended a large garden of almost any vegetable you imagine could grow in the northeast Iowa climate—corn, beans, cabbage, asparagus, potatoes, carrots, tomatoes, strawberries, cucumbers, ground cherries, and beets. Mom carved out, cultivated, and tended a large flower garden of poppies, daffodils, phlox, peonies, iris, lilies, and more. It must have been a ton of work for them, especially in spring and summer seasons with small children running about.

Later, while raising my family of three children, I attempted a meager garden in our side yard—maybe to somehow replicate the blissful fantasy world of those early years at The Green House—but my attention waned. Too many times, the broccoli and cauliflower went to seed before I claimed their offerings. I distracted myself with it—keeping busy kept the overwhelming feeling of loneliness I had at bay during those years. I wonder if keeping busy also helped Mom cope in the life she found herself in; a life not well planned or directed toward her own needs and desires. She gave all of herself to care for her family, neglecting herself in the process.

Although Mom was spread thin, we girls had each other. We all looked up to Colleen, the oldest and the ringleader and four years my senior. We followed her lead, even though her over-the-shoulder, eyebrow-furling glances solidified our unworthiness. The most timid of us all, Rhonda, followed Colleen in age. Many early group photos of us highlight Rhonda's wide-eyed, deer-in-the-headlights expression, and nary a conversation between us today goes by without some reference to how she'd leap onto the sofa as a scared cat might, screaming with terror when Mom got out the vacuum cleaner and roared it past her. Colleen and Rhonda didn't welcome Jill, the middle sister and fifteen months older than me, into their play. Having outgrown Kelly and my babyish entertainment, Jill did well straddling the center position and finding her space, establishing a number of outside friendships. Number four of the five, I didn't stand out. Inexplicably quiet a lot of the time, my sisters tell me I would not talk for hours, even when asked questions. We doted on Kelly, the youngest and only blond among us, at least for those first few years.

An ideal place for a kid, I have fond memories of The Green House. Situated on a V-shaped corner lot with a few acres of land and an old barn, I imagine it a parcel from a much larger property which long ago kept numerous farm animals and maybe some crops. Near the house stood the barn—a paved patio with a tire-anchored tether ball separating the two—complete with hay and dirt, as if the previous owner just walked out with a horse and cow and never looked back. But the salt lick, gray with grime and age, intrigued us the most. It became a constant item of temptation and the consequence of losing at "double dare ya" challenges. We whelped dog pups in the barn from Lady and Duchess, our German Shepherds, both eventual victims of the highway traffic south of the property line.

We made up games and relied on Colleen to tell us the rules—how we needed to "freeze" in place when the museum owner (usually her) swung us around in the yard to form her next sculpture in Swing-a-Statue, what "sickness" we had (usually a marble up the nose or cigarette butt in the ear) when we played Doctor (yes, Colleen was the doctor in residence).

We always did what Colleen said. One time, Jill, not wanting to miss out on a round of play, crouched down in the side yard after a win at freeze tag. "I have to go the bathroom," she said.

"Come here everyone," Colleen directed, waving us together with her arms. We gathered in a locked-arm circle around Jill as she pulled her underwear and pants down to pee in the grass, hoping not to gain the attention of any passing semi-tractor trailer driver or nosy neighbor driving by.

My simple, unsullied self, viewed the property's lawn as a vast, velvety expanse of Kentucky Blue Grass with hidden pockets of clover, frequently searched by giggling, competitive girls for that lucky four-leaf mutation. Lying among the cool blades on a warm June afternoon, Jill and I rolled our limber bodies—made stiff as logs with arms outstretched above our heads—down the gentle front yard slope. We were thoughtless to the grass stains, dirt, and potential spider mite bites we might be exposing our clothes, limbs, and bellies to. Breathless, we'd stop on our backs and contemplate the puffy, cotton ball clouds overhead. "That one looks like a dragon," I'd say. "Do you see the clown face in that one?" Jill would say. Earlier we had squealed in fear and revulsion at the four-inch green caterpillar found on a discarded maple leaf, its alien, segmented body lined with hairy orange and blue nobs.

The two-story, too-small-but-just-right house had a wonderfully open but dark, creepy basement (I swear it had dirt floors and, even if it didn't, smelled like a crypt), one bathroom and two bedrooms downstairs, and a satisfyingly open second floor with one small, enclosed room and a door to the attic.

Sitting at the laminate, metal-edged kitchen table on cracked vinyl chairs at lunchtime, I played with my macaroni and watched Colleen and Rhonda dare Jill to put her gray-green beans in the coal chute a step away from the table next to the basement stairs. "Do it! Do it!" they taunted, until Jill, desperate for their attention and good graces, jumped down and tossed a spoonful in the chute, hopping back in her chair in the nick of time, avoiding Mom's scolding before she came back into the room and saw our mischief.

Looking back, my childhood seemed idyllic, and—to many an outsider—it probably appeared so. Of course, we girls had our moments of disagreement—someone mysteriously punching out the face of Rhonda's new baby doll with a pen. Rhonda chasing Jill through the breezeway door and shattering the glass with her wrist, which led to the hysteria of us believing she was going to bleed to death. Colleen throwing a spade at Jill's head during another deadly pursuit. But we knew we had each other and followed each other's lead, playing together as sisters were supposed to do.

My basic needs were filled growing up—home cooking via southern-style, lard-laden meals; homestead-like, randomly-decorated shelter; home-sewn, inherited, and often matching hand-me-down dresses. Even with all this, my sisters were the ones to fill my needs for emotional connection. They were the ones I emulated and looked to when playing *In Search Of*, trying to find Mom after scraping my knee, or just needing a hug. I often wonder if Mom stood there somewhere, watching us play together from the kitchen window like June Cleaver, happily buffing the glassware she had just washed from lunch. My intuition says no.

I was four when we moved to The Green House. The older three sisters were in school at least half of the day, so Kelly (a year younger than me) and I were pals. We'd sit out at the picnic table, dare each other to eat Cat Chow, struggle to reach the tether ball and complete a full game, and play with Barbies and paper dolls together. Most days we would ride around and around and around in the garage on a tricycle, the Big Wheel, and the mini-sized John Deere tractor with George, the neighbor boy who lived two doors down the highway. George was my age, and we rode the school bus together to kindergarten. "My turn to ride the Big Wheel," I yelled to Kelly after doing my time on the slow tractor, making sure not to tip over trying to make the sharp turns required in the one-car garage. With the door closed, the tires crackled and spun on the dirty concrete as we sang our ABCs and nursery rhymes we'd learned by heart. Mom brought us Kool-Aid and bologna sandwiches, but we couldn't stop, or the Big Wheel driver would pass us.

One night Mom quietly walked up the stairs to our bedroom and peered around the banister. "Tracy, come down here for a minute," she said softly. I slowly and curiously followed her down the stairs to the living room, aglow from the light of the TV. Dad sat in his chair silently, watching the evening news per his nightly routine. I sat next to Mom on the sofa.

"Early this afternoon, a boy was hit and killed by a car on Highway 63 south of town. The boy was playing in his front yard and had apparently run out into the road after a ball," the anchorman said solemnly.

I looked back at Mom, still not understanding why she asked me to come downstairs. "It's George," she said, patting my back gently, but I wasn't sure what she meant. He was my first non-family friend—the first friend I was allowed to call on the off-white, rotary dial phone hanging on the kitchen wall, the only person I could count on to save me a seat on the bus after half-day kindergarten class. Death was not in my vocabulary, and I went to bed still not really understanding what the big deal was. Mom hugged me and sent me back to bed, confused.

Sitting in a cramped middle row of the funeral home, all I could see were the stiff suit jackets and dark skirts of adults' backsides all around me. I felt overshadowed, small, and invisible. I kept hearing George's name, some organ music, then it ended. I held Mom's hand as we slowly filed out of the pew, trying to pull her in the opposite direction of the crowd. But her lead was too strong and my will too weak. I was desperate to see if George was somewhere in the room. Everyone was talking about him, but I never found him there.

I don't remember talking about the loss of my friend to my mom or dad or anybody. Mom was gentle when sharing the news to me, but I don't recall death being explained to me, being asked about my feelings, or even talking about it to my parents after the event. I didn't act out and didn't regress in any way. I just remember being really confused and left to figure out this death "thing" on my own. I simply followed my parents' lead, going on about my life as before, as if nothing happened.

Yes, Mom was there for us growing up, keeping us fed and clothed, but my memory is of her as caretaker in physical form only. I don't remember any closeness with her, no tender moments being cherished or made to feel special or being listened to. At my age, though, this felt normal.

As an adult, I mentored teenage girls at risk of dropping out of school or entering the juvenile justice system. One girl's mother was a drug addict and formerly incarcerated. She had several children of various ages with multiple men. From my adult perspective, the child must despise her mother for not being there for her, for not taking care of herself so she could take care of her family. But that was not the case. At a holiday gathering, this girl walked around the crowded room clinging to her mother's arm, looking up at her with complete adoration, even as the mother nervously looked away at the door for an escape. I had just witnessed the power mothers have on their children, no matter what they put them through or how messed up their own lives are. As a child, my mom meant everything to me, too.

Many days, Mom would fold mounds of laundry on the tired arm of the living room sofa, watching soap operas for hours in the afternoons. Craving a scrap of attention or the faint upturn of a smile and nod, we sprawled on our stomachs on the gray matted Berber carpet, heads in hands, and watched them along with her. We learned about adult behavior and drama we certainly didn't learn from anyone else. Besides the dramatic music and passionate pleas of the TV characters, the room stayed quiet with not a word said among us. This was Mom's world, not meant for young girls. We somehow knew to tread carefully. In my mind, the living room was gray—gray carpet, gray walls, gray mood—matching the old black-and-white TV residing there. And not just on those drama-laced afternoons. Even my memories of Christmas—lighted tree, shredded wrapping paper, toys, and games—are in black and white, not enhanced by the large picture windows spanning both walls of the corner dining area.

Mom, often detached and sullen, would slam herself into her bedroom in the middle of the day, leaving us to our own devices, imagination, and caretaking. Once, she asked eight-year-old Colleen if she wanted to learn to cook and gave her a blue box of macaroni and cheese to make for us all, as Mom shut herself in her bedroom again. Here's when Jill learned to blow milk from her nose, Rhonda got an electric shock from the broken toaster, and we shoveled overcooked green beans down the coal chute.

Frosted Flakes or other sugar-coated cereals and goodies were not a luxury we experienced back then, but we found a way to get our sugar fix. Holding our breath and peering apprehensively into the well-lit kitchen from the living room, we watched Jill tiptoe to the counter, stealthily pull the silverware drawer and lift out a spoon with two fingers. "Shhhh!" Colleen motioned with finger to lips while looking down the hall to Mom's bedroom door. Jill quietly licked the spoon and jabbed it into the glass sugar bowl next to the coffee percolator, scampering back to us, reward in hand. We all took a lick at the white, crack-like substance, and idolized Jill for her bravery.

Most Sundays we attended Mass at historic St. Joseph's Catholic Church in downtown Waterloo. The voluminous church echoed with cries of what must have been at least a couple other children, maybe babies, although they just might have been my own. My feet were curled beneath me as I sat on the hard, wooden pew, everyone else standing at attention, no doubt to some "up" part of the "up down, up down" practice accepted in Catholic Masses across the globe. I probably looked as if I had just been beaten with my wet, reddened face, tears and snot streaming down in rivers and dripping on the orange painted curve of the seat. On the back of the pew in front of us hung pockets with hymnals and small envelopes and short little pencils without erasers. As I scribbled with one of those pencils on one of those envelopes, Mom grabbed my hand with an angry squeeze and irate expression, forcing me to let go of both. A deep shame and sadness overcame me as she callously grabbed a hymnal and stood up with the others, the rejection stinging painfully for the remaining service and the entire ride home in the back of the station wagon. There's a deep aloneness inside me when I think of this event, even today. I lost a part of myself there but am confused as to what it was.

Today when I swing, I get dizzy and sick, no doubt a foreboding of my longing to return to my early days in the side yard of The Green House. Things have changed since then. I am still compelled to do a drive-by during those more and more infrequent visits to Waterloo, trying to conjure up those good days with the smell of the sun, and the laughter and naiveté. The house is pale yellow now. The gravel road behind the house paved, the field across the street once comforting an old horse now corrals seniors in an assisted living facility. The highway bordering the south property line no longer rumbles with deadly eighteen-wheelers since the Highway 63 bypass rerouted them in the mid-1970s. The house and property have changed quite a bit, as decades of time do to things, but my memories are strong, warm, melancholy of the good times, the best times I ever remember with my sisters and family growing up.

DICK AND MARY

"Children are naturally compassionate and loving and tend to try to meet parents' needs. But it is not our job, not our job [as children] to fill our parents' needs."
—DIANE POOLE HELLER, *HEALING YOUR ATTACHMENT WOUNDS*

My mother, Mary Juanita Hulstine—born to grade-school educated, sharecropping parents at the height of the Dust Bowl in Norman, Oklahoma—spent her early years lonely. Transient and destitute, the impoverished family of nine lacked nearly everything a household that size needed to prosper. The dirt floor homes she spent chasing her younger brothers in were well-used shanties, without running water or electricity or, most-likely, even windows. Leaving the one-room schoolhouses for planting season in the spring, Mary and her siblings left school before completing their grade and fell behind in their education. Maybe even more devastating, they left behind any new, budding friendships beginning to develop. Mary's older sister and brother spent time together and helped with chores, so Mary hung around her younger brothers, becoming a tomboy in the process.

After bearing seven children, Mary's mother learned she had a uterine tumor and should not get pregnant again, but either lacking in resources or maybe understanding of basic human conception, she did. As a youth, Mary suffered several bouts of pneumonia. "I can save the girl but not the mother," the doctor said to the family after being called out to the house one day and before ordering them both to the hospital. At just ten years old and bedridden with the disease, Mary watched her mother hemorrhage to death in the hospital bed beside her. She wondered if it was really her mom next to her as she floated in and out of consciousness that day. Mary's younger brother, just six at the time, hesitated when recalling this period of his life: "Mom was buried in a cemetery across the road from our one-room schoolhouse. We weren't allowed to go the funeral, but we looked out the window at her grave site every day."

Mary's father, Charles, could not manage seven children ages one to fifteen after their mother passed, and the family split up. The two youngest—ages one and three at the time— were adopted by his brother and wife. Mary and the other four were left with Charles, forsaking the "opportunities" of sharecropping—which were non-existent by then—and moving to Texas where he had family. Charles hopped from job to job, and those next few, unstructured years before he re-married were times of isolation and independence for children mourning the loss of their mother and needing guidance, nurturing, and emotional support. The family eventually settled in Atlanta, Texas, where Charles found steady work at a sawmill. He married a severe woman who cooked and watched over the children but drove them away with her spiteful comments and demeanor.

Tired of living with two pesky younger brothers, a strict, verbally abusive stepmother, and an asshole for a father, Mom abandoned school at seventeen despite good grades and with just a few months until graduation. In her boat-necked cotton shirt and fitted knee-length pants, she wrapped her shoulder-length dark hair in a ponytail with a flowered scarf and grabbed a small but bulky suitcase. She marched away from the three-room shack home in Atlanta, never looking back, as her best girlfriend of the same name waited in the yard. They set off down the dusty road with their thumbs out, smiling sweetly and cursing the cars grazing too close, pelting them with rocks and debris as they passed without stopping, destination Miami. Seven years and two divorces later, Mary found herself in 1961 living with her older sister in Kansas after running out of money and places to escape. What happened in those seven years remains a mystery to her daughters. Later when watching her far-away eyes reminisce, we knew they were adventure-filled, once-in-lifetime escapades of a couple of young women shunning the restrictive lifestyles imposed upon them by overworked and overburdened families.

Born Richard Lee Anderson, my dad's family called him Dick and friends called him Andy. With Conway Twitty-Brylcreemed hair, Dad saw everyone as a friend. Old photos show a tall, thin grinning teenager posing to catch a football, a younger version of him I didn't know but often wished I were friends with. He grew up on a small, Northeast Iowa farm to spare-the-rod-spoil-the-child Catholic parents. The strict household was not without love, but my grandmother kept tight reins on her children, enforcing their ultimate salvation through repeated licks of a belt, when necessary. The eldest of five children and dearly loved and respected by his siblings, Dick enlisted in the US Army after high school.

Dick met Mary while on leave as she waited tables at a busy, Manhattan, Kansas, bar. Tall, slim, attractive

Mary—with her teased hair and snappy attitude—and tall, blue-eyed, quick-witted Dick made a good-looking, amiable pair. For whatever reason, Dick ran late picking Mary up at the bar on their first planned date. Mary sat cross-legged at the dimly lit bar, idly stirring her "last call" vodka tonic, Marty Robbins playing on the jukebox in the background.

"What have you got going tonight, Bobby?" Mary commented with a sigh to her bartender coworker, making small talk.

"Nothing much. Got an early—" Bobby began, when they were interrupted by the abrupt opening of the bar door.

Dick skidded through the door, throwing his green Army Garrison cap in the center of the room.

Mary rolled her eyes and laughed, "It's about time." Apology accepted.

Just months after they met, Mary found herself at Thanksgiving dinner in La Porte City, Iowa, with Dick's family, introducing herself as his new bride after a hasty wedding-of-necessity a few miles away. "Estle, would you say the blessing, please?" Dick's mother, Agnes, said tersely to her husband, after she sat down. The hand-carved coo-coo clock hanging on the wall ticked off the seconds, but no one noticed through the thick air.

"Dick, pass your sister the dressing," Agnes instructed, reaching past Mary to hand Dick the bowl. Agnes barely acknowledged Mary. Mary remained quiet as she passed turkey, mashed potatoes, and beans to Dick's family. She smiled politely through the awkward silence and matter-of-fact conversation, wondering just what she had gotten herself into with this commitment. Familiar with the judging eyes of a mother figure, she equated Agnes' disdain with her stepmother's that she knew well.

Devoted Catholic Agnes refused to look Mary in the eye but forgave her eldest child's adulterous transgression and accepted his self-absolution. Eventually over those first few years, Agnes would patiently teach Mary to sew and cook Dick's favorite meals. Several years later and after a lengthy process of annulling her first marriage, Mary dutifully joined the Catholic church, and her mother-in-law offered her full acceptance.

For the first few years, Mary and Dick got by on a soldier's stipend and then an apprentice's salary. As the children kept coming—five daughters in six years—times were tight, but they were able to rent a small house on the edge of Waterloo. The family received hand-me-down clothes from family and friends, and Mary learned to sew, alter, and mend everything she and her family wore. Dick's family shared their garden surplus with the young couple, and Mary learned to cook.

Young and beautiful, Mom transitioned to the settled, domestic, mother-of-five life. As chaotic as it must have been, it didn't compare to the rebellious, individualistic life she lived traversing the country with her girlfriend. But she adopted this life, turning her full attention to her daughters— at least at first—cooking, cleaning, sewing, making sure meals were on the table routinely morning, noon, and night. She embraced the life of her new husband, hundreds of miles away from her own family, rarely talking to or about them, assimilating as a good wife aught. Even with her husband's family and her own growing family for company, Mom—by her own volition—remained isolated, solitary and separate, polite and amiable, but guarded and protected.

A few years later and before I entered kindergarten, Mom wanted to work nights to bring in extra money. She didn't have a driver's license, so she started taking lessons. Arriving back home after dropping Mom off at her class, Dad tied a short apron around his waist, opened a couple cans of Van Camp's Pork and Beans into a saucepan, and turned on the stove burner. Curious to watch six-foot, two-inch Dad in the kitchen, we twirled and danced around behind him trying to stay out of his way as he diced hot dogs and warmed a can of green beans for our supper.

The evening light faded as we sat at the supper table wiggling in our chairs scooping beanie-weenie into our mouths. "Finish up. Your mother's about done with her class," Dad announced, looking at his watch nervously. Compliantly we shoved the remaining spoonfuls in our mouths and took our plates to the sink, where Colleen helped dry dishes as fast as Dad could wipe them off.

Giggling, we crammed into the station wagon. "Settle down, girls," Dad reminded us sternly, but our collective singing, "We're almost there! We're almost there!" couldn't be stifled. We rolled around in the back seat, leaning on each other through turns and poking at Colleen in the front seat.

When Dad's sister agreed to babysit us girls, Mom and Dad headed to Vic's Lounge, their hangout and date night destination. Vic's was a friendly bar they discovered near the first two places they were able to rent as a young couple. Mom and Dad became quick friends with the owners and regular patrons of the family-owned establishment. When Mom got her driver's license, she started working there a few nights a week. Vic's offered Mom the opportunity to make good tips and socialize with familiar faces.

Drunken fights were the norm when Mom made it home after work. Those nights the five of us sat cringing on the warped, wooden planks of the house's narrow staircase with our thin, pilled nightgowns stretched over our legs, knees pulled to our chins. We couldn't see their interaction, but the dry, chilly air, crisp with apprehension fueled our fear and anxiety, removing any sense of safety and security we might have imagined and coveted.

"I don't see why you have to work there!" Dad shouted. "You should be here, looking after the girls, instead of flirting with all the drunks. I see how they look at you!"

"You're just jealous," Mom laughed with a slur, feebly pushing him away with one hand.

Wide-eyed and barely breathing, we'd scuttle back to our beds when Dad walked by—Mom passed out in his arms— barking "Get back in bed, girls!" Dad's jealousy over Mom's flirtations ended the short-lived night shift at Vic's.

Over their forty-eight-year marriage—at least the part I witnessed—I don't remember other verbal fights except for those early years. Dick came home to supper dutifully at 4:45 p.m. each night, slapping Mom on the ass remarking, "Hey, Fat Texan. What's for supper?" although no one could ever label Mom as plump. Terse pecks on the cheek and dutiful smiles aside, I also don't remember tremendous outpourings of affection and tenderness between them either. Sometimes I'd hear the bathroom door bang shut late at night, and as an adult, I surmised physical intimacy between them (but even that I struggled to consider).

For unknown reasons, I took it as my responsibility to placate the tension between Mom and Dad—and in the household in general—playing "peacemaker" and "good girl." I measured my success through "conscientious and diligent" remarks on my straight-A report cards. I became an expert at reading a room, slipping in under the radar during lighter times, and providing a positive diversion when even a Ginsu knife couldn't cut the air. No wonder my sisters labeled me the golden child—I had to play the perfect child part so things wouldn't fall apart emotionally for anyone in the room.

For me, finally setting out to college as a teenager allowed an escape from the perpetual household tension. All of us left home as soon as we could, never looking back. One adult manifestation of childhood emotional neglect is remembering one's childhood as lonely even if happy, but my childhood had obvious good times. My selective, vain memory had me believe Mom and Dad didn't care what I did in college, never asking about grades, career plans, personal life, too wrapped up in their own unhappiness to notice. But that rested in my own head. Years later in my attic I found a pile of treasured notes they mailed me during my first year at Iowa State University, part of the school's first-year student support program where parents could encourage their child and fight homesickness and dropouts. So, it seems they cared and did think of me (us). Doing it long distance through a third-party was just easier than breaking the icy wall of detachment permeating interactions of my childhood.

As an adult I avoided calling or checking in with my parents. I knew I "needed to" or "should," but for some reason I dreaded any interchange. Father's Day one year, Mom called us all out for not sending Dad anything for the day or even reaching out to him. (I had sent a card, but he would not get it until the Monday after the holiday.) I'm ashamed about this and the many missed connections with them, especially Dad, and the multiple times I picked up the phone to call them only to put it back down again.

DAISY

"People pleasing behaviors evolve as a way to maintain con-nection and closeness with parents who are inconsistently available to their children."
—ANN STONESON, "WHAT MAKES A PEOPLE PLEASER"

I called my dad "Daisy"—a sloppy "Daddy" from a young tot's mouth—which established my position as "daddy's favorite" in the annals of The Anderson Girls' saga. "Boo, come over here and take my boots off, will ya?" he'd say, more of a command than request as he pumped the handle to the reclining position on his obedient La-Z-Boy. I'd duti-fully kneel on the green shag carpet, newly combed to stiff attention with the carpet rake. "Boo," his nickname for me, became one that close friends and my husband have taken way too seriously, preventing me from burying it with my youth. I didn't dislike the pet name—I perked up and bright-ened when Dad used it. But somehow it stings a little when friends and sisters use it today.

I guess I always knew of my special relationship with Dad, but I didn't realize his attention focused on just me.

I assumed my sisters felt this way about Dad, enjoyed the same consideration from him that I did. It stung, and I must have flinched when in my forties I learned they labeled me GC ("the golden child") because of this favored status. I pretended not to acknowledge the privileged relationship; we all craved the focused attention of at least one adult more than the scraps we received and hungrily accepted like characters in Dante's hell.

I have fond memories of helping Dad with yard work growing up. The riding mower roared as it bumped along the unending expanse of lawn, whipping up dust particles and fueling the unforgettable scent of fresh-cut grass I willingly inhaled. My butt took the brunt of the adventure, numb from the vibrating, shiny green wheel cover I perched on. Hanging on to Dad's ever-expanding midsection, we'd swivel around the random, botanical garden–like selection of trees dotting the front yard. Dad would point at a branch in front of us and slow the machine to a halt. I'd jump down, pick it up and throw it in the compost bin or mulch pile. Chasing him down again, I would see Jill come out of the house waving her arms in declaring it her turn for a ride. But I'd outrun her and jump back on, looking back in triumph.

Sitting dutifully at our sibling-assigned supper table spots one summer night, the nightly news rambled on behind us, Salisbury steak and mashed potatoes with gravy on our Green Stamp plates. Dad bestowed on me twenty-five dollars for mowing the entire acre lawn with the push mower without being told.

"I mowed the lawn last week and didn't get a thing for it! Why does she get paid for doing it?" cried Jill to Dad's deaf ears. Lawn mowing became a competitive business between us girls. I sheepishly accepted the cash, ignoring the disparity of opportunity among us girls in this regard.

Along with mowing the lawn, Dad and I had our routine around the house. Walking down the narrow hall in his yellow-stained and armpit-crusty V-neck T-shirt on Saturday mornings, Dad would say, "Come on, Boo." I'd jump to attention from my prone position in front of TV cartoons, agreeably following him down to his basement man cave of a woodworking corner where treasured tools awaited his attention to complete some required household repair. I'd skip down the bowed basement steps behind him, through the damp, musty washroom and grab any item he thought he might need for the day's chore—hammer, screwdriver, entire red Craftsman toolbox.

Being the professional tinkerer that he was, he also had a garage full of neatly organized man toys—garden tools, a rototiller, a Weed Eater, and apparatuses to either repel or attract the dog-size squirrels littering the yard. Dad enjoyed his "stuff," maybe as more of an escape from a loveless marriage than serving any serious need. In hindsight, I'm grateful for these times with Dad and the opportunity to learn how to use basic household tools, the proper way to hold and swing a hammer, the difference between a flat-head and cross-point screwdriver, the many uses of pliers. Putting a nail through a two-by-four in three swell swings satisfies like nothing else, and I didn't have to learn it from an Ace Hardware video.

At seven years old, this special bond I had with Dad suffered a blow. I had been allowed to wash his back when he bathed in the evenings, but I guess an age comes for all of us when innocent behaviors of young children become uncomfortable to adults. As Dad sat hunched over in soapy, inches-deep water, the drip of the faucet breaking the echo-ing bathroom's silence, I bounded in to suds up his back for him, a privilege bestowed on me and my sisters since we were tots. This demonstrated an unspoken act of love and caring, an honor to be able to attend to Dad in this way.

As I stood barefoot on the small shag rug in my paja-mas and lathered up the washcloth, Mom walked in and interrupted, saying, "You're too old for this anymore." She handed me a towel and pointed to the door with a nod. I looked back as she shuffled me out of the humid room. Not saying a word or even looking at me, Dad had picked up the washcloth himself and had begun to suds up his arm as if nothing happened. My insides shriveled. My heart ached. Thinking Dad didn't want me around anymore, I sat stunned and dejected on the living room sofa in silence for a long time. I took this new development as a sign Dad no longer wanted me, no longer saw me as part of the spe-cialness I must have been, I had to be. I don't know why this little event stung so much or why it seemed to change things between Dad and me. I didn't understand then, and there's still a piece of that wound still healing within me. I guess rejection stings at any age and sometimes it pierces so deeply it stays with you a lifetime.

My sisters and I remember a regularly active, athletic Dad when we were young. He took part in volleyball, basketball, and bowling leagues regularly. Kelly and I particularly would sit on the backless benches swinging our legs and listening to the rubber-soled squeaks on the high-glossed, wood plank gym floor. We'd watch Dad's volleyball league game at the new junior high school in town. I remember the feeling of excitement and belonging; the acknowledgement and the adventure of getting out of the house in the evening seemed special. I'm not sure how long Dad did this, but these were early memories of a man with drive, health, interests, and friendly connections. Where did this go? When did this end? Why did this end?

Whatever the reason, I jumped at chances in our rural elementary school's "Olympics" to show my athleticism in the high jump and hurdles, knowing sports assured Dad's attention and favor. Throughout junior high and high school, I participated in every sport I could—tennis, track, volleyball, and basketball—and Dad attended nearly all my high school basketball games, both home and away.

"Put your glasses on, ref!" I heard Dad's voice from the raucous crowd after being called for a foul and leveled by the forward coming in for a layup. I looked up to see him leaning forward, thick eyebrows furled, shaking his head.

Walking out of the locker room after the loss, I headed to Dad talking with my coach about the game. "Good game," Coach said.

"You'll get 'em next time, Boo," Dad said, putting his arm on my shoulder and leading me out of the empty gym's door.

I know living some of his life too on that court solidified our connection and my feeling of doing the right thing, following the right rules. I don't remember Mom attending any games, but it didn't bother me. She wasn't the one I was trying to make happy again.

Being athletic in junior high and high school helped me feel justified. I used it to prove myself and please and gain favor from Dad. I relate to Rich Roll in his memoir *Finding Ultra* where he says that he didn't have any special skills. He was a nerd and a geek, but he could endure pain through swimming. As an adult I continue that internal need to feel justified and okay, even attempting to run a marathon through pain and injury. I didn't feel the acceptance and love I needed except from sports, didn't have any other special skills, but I knew I could endure pain.

Beyond athletic activities, my younger dad was also an outdoorsman and loved fishing and hunting. At age five or six, I last joined him on a men's trip to a dusty, heatless cabin with five or six men smelling of dirt, sweat, and cigarette smoke. Old photos show men swaddled tight in army-green sleeping bags, lying on bunks against bare-wood walls. At the table in the common room during poker games, I'd sit on Dad's lap and take sips of his Budweiser. I looked up at him for his approval, and he'd raise an eyebrow while moving the can away from my reach. I leaned back into his chest as I held his cards. "Which one, Dad?" I'd say, tilting my head up and back to look at him. He'd wink and point to the card he wanted me to play.

I laid it down, and he teased, "Keep your cards close. Roy cheats!" bringing my card-filled hands to my chest as Roy protested. Somehow through the raucous laughing and outbursts, I belonged there with Dad—his sidekick, the son he never had. Then it stopped, and these trips no longer included me.

Trying to find my way in life through Dad, these moments affected me a lot. By pleasing him, enjoying the same things he enjoyed, I would find my happiness and the "right" way to live. I didn't have to risk trying anything for myself; I just needed to follow his lead, his direction. I don't remember having separate ideas on how I wanted to live or what I wanted to do. It always reflected what Dad wanted, or what would make Dad happy.

Sometime in my early teens, Dad purchased a red Lund aluminum fishing boat which grandly took up half the self-built garage space and displaced his pick-up truck to the brutal Iowa seasons. We could find him inside it cleaning, preening, waxing for an entire week before our annual fishing trip to Bowstring Lake in Minnesota, our only family vacation most years. With Merle Haggard crooning honkytonk from the AM radio station, Dad emerged from the sixteen-footer's bowels, throwing me the bow end of the thick, tan leather cover. "Hold on a minute, Boo. Let me get this laid out." Careful with his instructions, he made sure I didn't move until directed. Together we stretched, pulled, and forced the snaps into place until the vessel could be secured for the trip.

Just before dark that evening, Dad put the rotating water sprinkler on a spot of lawn and, at dark a couple hours later, we girls were out there with flashlights and buckets of dirt. Jill and I squatted as she shined her light on a spot of grass, and I perched, ready to grab an unsuspecting nightcrawler before it retracted back into the damp earth. I squealed at my first attempt at grabbing the slimy, slippery worm, and it got away. We moved a few feet over and found another, but this one snapped in two as I too aggressively yanked it out of its home. We screamed in disgust.

"Shhhh!" Dad barked. "You're scaring them all away." Dad never wanted to stop and purchase bait for the trip we could easily bring from home. Dad patiently demonstrated how to hold the worm taut and firm and wait for it to naturally ease itself out of the ground so we could add to our provision.

Growing up this way, I confidently handled and hooked earthworms or minnows and expertly lifted a sunfish up out of the water, grabbing it and taking the hook out of its lip. Dad showed us how. Summer Saturday mornings he'd wake us up at dawn to remove little green cabbage worms from our garden before they could do much damage or pluck potatoes out of the ground as he dug them up before it got too hot. My sisters grumbled about this. I would have preferred sleeping in those mornings, too, but if Dad asked me to help, I did, just because he asked.

From this relationship I first came to know being the good girl, doing what I was told, and keeping the peace was the way to favor and "rightness" in the world. I learned if I stayed in the lines, didn't upset Mom or Dad (or any adult, for that matter), got good grades, didn't make a fuss, went along, then that was the lane to stay in. I persistently looked to others to find my way, give me direction, be my weather vane to the world. I didn't look inward for what I wanted and needed because I was driven to please the adults in my world. I didn't learn to push boundaries, that of others or myself. I didn't experiment or try new things. I did everything I could to stay within what I thought were life's tried and true boundaries for living.

When my widowed mother ended up living so close to me as an adult, this "making everyone happy" persona did me in. I tried hard to please her, make her happy, do what she wanted me to do the way I did with Dad. But I had no idea how to do this for her. Winning that game and keeping my sanity became impossible. But I tried.

EAST SHAULIS ROAD

———

"We are only capable of passing on or giving what we have received."

—ANITA OOMMEN, *PICKING UP THE SHARDS*

If someone would have asked me, "Were you loved?" during my childhood, I would have said, "Yes." We always had food on the table, parents who stayed together and rarely fought outwardly with each other. Besides the occasional spankings with a yardstick doled out equally among us girls when justified, I endured no physical abuse. I had no reason to think I wasn't loved or cared for. But something was missing. Lying on my back across the iron-framed bed I shared with Kelly as a teenager, hair in a tangled mess as my head dangled off the side, I called out weakly, "Help. Help. Help me." But I remained alone, no rescuer in sight. My home environment lacked an element of caring concern for me and the developing person I was becoming. It left me hanging, unfulfilled, unsatisfied.

In the early years living on East Shaulis Road in Waterloo, Iowa, I had recurring ruminations, daydreams, of being alone in the world, in a bubble, the only human with feelings and emotions. In this existence, I was a nothing, forgotten and forlorn, the only one who cared or actually bled. A specimen studied, observed, and toyed with, I saw everyone else—every other "human" in the world—as a robot, controlled by an overarching, central deity, to study and probe my humanness. I've often wondered if these were just normal thoughts of a child's growing ego, a stage of self-concept recognized in Erik Erikson's psychosocial development theory. I've since learned when children are neglected emotionally—when parents fail to respond enough to a child's emotions—they think they are all alone, separate from others. It's called childhood emotional neglect (CEN) and is an unmemorable childhood experience, but it is powerful and happens daily—subliminally and under the radar. "The child receives the message: Your emotions are not important, not relevant, or not welcome here in your childhood home," says clinical psychologist Jonice Webb in a 2018 website article. Whatever the cause, the feeling of solitude and isolation still separates me from others and affects how I interact with adults to this day.

During those years living in the orange brick house on East Shaulis Road before I left for college at eighteen, I first recognize, in hindsight, glimpses of an internal emptiness, hollowness, shaping the background of much of my adult life. For some reason the good times are harder to remember, but they certainly existed. Mom and Grandma used to make us fabulous birthday cakes of elaborate castles with upturned ice cream cones for towers, butterflies with gumdrop wings and black licorice antennae, and even ones made with Barbies in southern belle-style gowns. Dad spent Christmas days putting together bicycles and racetracks, demonstrating how to use a pogo stick or jump around on a Bouncy Ball without losing our balance. We learned to water-ski and catch fish on our annual family fishing trips to Minnesota. These were great times and by many accounts idyllic, but children need more than a genial relationship with parents and adults as they grow up—more than a warm house, clothing, and three square meals.

In 1972 and in the middle of my first-grade year, we moved to the big, ranch-style house on the south side of town. Just before Christmas, the naked room where we erected the tree in front of large curtain-less windows echoed with our squeals of excitement. As Mom and Dad hauled boxes into the house, my sisters and I performed cartwheels throughout the bare home. We ran breathless from room to room, inaugurating each with a series of flips, headstands and arms-extended "ta-das." To us, the expanse was intentional, a dedicated training facility to practice our budding gymnastic skills. It was eventually filled with beds, tables, and shelves. The large 2,000-square-foot house sat on an acre lot and had an open floor basement the original owners had built like a bomb shelter and lived in long before the main floor could be completed. The house had three bedrooms (four if you included the office off the kitchen), one and a half baths, a separate dining room, a family room, and a living room—plenty of space for all of us, at least "us" as little girls.

The unfinished concrete-floor dungeon had a small bathroom and shower, old refrigerator and stove, and small shelved closet Mom used as a canning cellar. Perfect for riding bikes in the winter and hosting junior high school parties, it housed several families of presumptuous wolf spiders. A couple of times each summer we'd scurry down there peeking out the twelve-inch hopper windows at the dark sky and branches blowing by, as Dad tuned in on his transistor radio to the news of where the latest tornadoes were tracking. As we grew older and desperate for more privacy, we created bedrooms in the dank space, separated by makeshift shower curtain walls and discarded dressers. Colleen and I would jump on the old sofa and chairs banished there, singing our lungs out to Elton John and Kiki Dee's "Don't Go Breaking My Heart."

We had a large garden at the back of the house. Made up of mostly vegetables, I remember hoeing potatoes, pulling carrots, picking strawberries, and biting into sour, green apples before they were fully ripe. In the summer months we shucked corn, snapped beans, pitted cherries, and shelled peas. Sitting in the side yard Kentucky bluegrass in a folding aluminum chair in the late afternoon shade of the house, I lifted my head to the warm summer breeze on my face, listening to the leaves rustle in the wind, the smell of sunshine wafting by. We talked frequently at the supper table about the great harvest of all the produce from my parents' efforts, how many tomatoes Mom canned and when the corn would be ready to pick. The garden held promise and regularity of success. Dad worked with his rototiller. Mom spent her days baking fresh rhubarb pie, canning tomatoes, or fermenting cabbage for sauerkraut in the hallway.

Grandma and Grandpa Anderson lived thirty minutes away from us, in a small white house on the main road into their town. I cherished sitting on Grandpa's lap and sneaking a peek in his front shirt pocket as he bounced his knee up and down. Leaning my head on his shoulder, he smelled of tobacco and dirt. "What's in your pocket, Grandpa?" I'd say with a grin and a bat of my eyelids, knowing he always hid candy there for his grandkids.

He'd grin and tease, "Nothing," covering the opening with his hand. Grandpa slurped when he spoke. I'd giggle trying to pull his fingers apart to access the orange marsh-mallow circus peanuts or French burnt peanuts candy he hid there. I've always longed to be a grandfather just like him, something I knew I could never be. I felt safe there with him, different than how I felt at my own home lacking in affection or playfulness.

Damp and musty, with its painted concrete floor, their basement became my favorite spot in the house. It held a plethora of interesting things—old photos, toys, blankets, cans, and jars—and I remember it as a place I could escape and color in the dozens of activity and coloring books Grandma kept down there. I would color for hours—in the lines of course—always a structure to this play. Sometimes I would color all the scenes with girls. Next, I would color all the scenes with dogs. And sometimes I couldn't skip around the book, I had to color the first page, then second and so on—always a system and process. I just couldn't understand why my cousin would just scribble in the books and ruin the pictures. Didn't she know the rules were to keep the colors within the lines? A few years before she passed, after she moved from her house into a nearby assisted living facility, Grandma mailed me a page from one of the coloring books she still had in her basement, one with my name on it in grade-school handwriting. Although strict and with firm boundaries, no one mistook Grandma's care and love for her grandchildren, something I questioned in my own home.

The eventual forty-eight-home neighborhood we moved to seemed randomly plopped in the middle of a corn and bean field a couple of miles south of the Waterloo "metrop-olis." The Guernsey Addition bragged streets named for dif-ferent breeds of cattle—Jersey, Angus, Charolais. My sisters hung out with the dozen or so neighbor kids who also lived there, running around away from our house a lot of the time, but there were just two boys my age in the neighborhood.

In my preteen years, I played Barbies for hours in the basement of Kelly's younger friend, Lyn. Her basement became "Barbie and Ken City," with Barbie home, Barbie closet (the size of a Barbie City block), Barbie roads for Ken's convertible, and Barbie's cousin, Francie's, house nearby. We had Barbies at our house, but Barbie World occupied Lyn's basement for an entire summer. "Can I play Barbies in your basement?" I'd ask Lyn's mom, when Kelly and Lyn were out doing God-knows-what in the neighborhood. With a roll of her eyes, she'd let me in where I'd play for hours by myself.

One day I asked Kelly, "Do you want to go over and play Barbies at Lyn's?" She scoffed and looked me up and down. Out of nowhere, Barbies were beneath my younger sister. I had not yet outgrown the childish amusement, and a hot shame swelled up inside me. But I craved the escape to a fantasy life, away from the too-silent home with Mom where I could come and go as I pleased, unnoticed.

Mom worked hard for us cooking, washing, and folding clothes, picking up after us. This was her life. Too rarely we'd catch her in the kitchen as she started supper, turning up the radio to the latest Elvis song. She'd snap her fingers, bend her elbows, and sway her jean-shorts clad hips to the tune, smiling to us mischievously. These few seconds of fun endeared us to our mother, but were too seldom witnessed.

She used to read interesting and cerebral books from Leon Uris, James Michener, and Carl Sagan. At one point, keen on astrology, she gave each of us readings based on our dates and times of birth. Later she moved to reading Harlequin romance novels and other light fiction. During summer and on weekends when my sisters were gallivanting around the neighborhood, I'd clean the house from top to bottom, vacuuming sofa cushions and beneath chairs and tables, wiping baseboards, ceiling fans, and even alphabetizing books on shelves. I managed my boredom this way, but deep down I tried to please Mom, ease her burden, possibly even make her smile. The home's windows revealed a warm, sunny, alive world, but only gray, sullen stillness endured inside.

One afternoon I put my ear to Mom and Dad's bedroom door, trying to tell if Mom was sleeping. "Yes?" came the exasperated response received after knocking warily. I opened the door to Mom laying on her side atop the covers, backside to me but head and shoulders turned in my direction.

"What is it?" she said crisply.

"Can Wendy sleep over tonight?" I asked.

Mom sighed loudly and looked up at the ceiling, seemingly irritated by the question. "Weren't you just over at her house?"

"On Thursday," I acknowledged.

"I suppose. But I'm not going over to pick her up. Now close the door and leave me alone. I'm trying to sleep." Afternoon naps were common for her and served the incessant somber mood of the home. Now, along with feeling alone and gloomy, a pit had developed in my stomach for waking her up.

I remember instances where I doubt she cared or knew what I was doing. One of my best friends in elementary school, Jamie, lived a half mile outside the neighborhood, down the gravel road. She raised pigs and sheep, showing them at FFA and 4-H fairs around the state. Once, a pig she named after me won a blue ribbon at the state fair. I remember walking through the shoulder-high ditch weeds over to her house, getting pelted with gravel and dust as pick-up trucks barreled down the road past me. I'm not sure Mom ever realized where I was, either shut in her bedroom or deep into her solitaire game, sipping southern-sweetened iced tea and filling the ashtray with crumpled butts.

Jamie and I were good friends but quite different. She had the strongest, longest fingernails of anyone I had ever seen and painted them different colors. Jamie, the baby of the family with two grown sisters, essentially grew up as the only child of two older parents. She seemed confident and outgoing; maybe that's what drew me to her. At the Hoover Junior High School lunch table, she and other friends would pass out nominal gifts on our respective birthdays. "Do you like it?" Jamie said, after watching me open her gift—a small figurine of a mouse playing the clarinet—her face puzzled by my expressionless facade. Touched by her thoughtfulness—I had started playing the clarinet that year in band—I didn't know how to accept such a gift, couldn't even find the feeling inside me to express my appreciation at having been seen, even in this infinitesimally small way by my preteen friend.

"Thank you," I said hesitantly, not looking at her, embarrassed and self-conscious. I never felt like a good friend, but the rodent clarinetist stayed on the wall shelf in my old bedroom until we moved Mom out after Dad died well into my forties.

One summer between my sophomore and junior years in high school, I invited another friend, Laurie, to the Minnesota fishing resort we frequented during our annual family fishing trips. Determined to leave our childhoods behind, we punked-out the neglected Barbies we brought with us, shaving and dying their hair and ratting out their denim skirts before performing a ceremonious burial at sea. Laurie and I leaned into our oars and pushed off the muddy lake floor, careful not to capsize the canoe among the shoreline cattails, loons croaking in the distance.

"As a symbol of our passage into adulthood, let these burning bodies open the gateway to a new worldview, a new outlook, a brighter future," Laurie pronounced, as I set the dolls' hair on fire with Mom's BIC lighter. We set the tokens of our childhood on make-shift rafts floating off in the mucky lake waters. In our minds this ritual completed our passage to maturity, promising each other solidarity in denying the pressures to fit in and be someone we weren't. We pledged to weather the last couple of years of high school, and we did.

Laurie became my sole confidant in those years, but she doesn't remember the afternoon later that year sitting cross-legged, knee-to-knee on her attic bedroom floor when I shared the despair I felt. "Do you ever feel like just going to sleep and never waking up?" I asked her. To this day I don't know what she said or how she said it. Maybe just her presence and being able to share this thought with her relieved me of something I never before let break the surface of pain I felt in my teenage years. I never seriously contemplated suicide—after all, it's a mortal sin for a "good" Catholic girl—but I did just want to check out, go to sleep, make it all go away. Whatever the exchange between Laurie and me that day, being heard relieved me of this oppressive burden, at least temporarily. Stephen Hayes, in his book, *A Liberated Mind*, suggests adolescent suicidal ideation is the mind trying to solve the problem of feeling bad inside. Whatever the reason for my melancholy, depression continued to follow me into my adult years.

The companionship and responsibility of a pet only exacerbated my feelings of isolation. Like the German Shepherds we had at The Green House, Dad enjoyed having dogs around and brought a Siberian Husky puppy home one weekend. We named him Nikki, short for "Nikita of the North." Not sure if a gift of some kind, Nikki was my dog, my responsibility, and I was to feed, brush, and exercise this inexhaustible beast. In the basement workshop, Dad and I followed instructions he found in one of his woodworking magazines and built and painted a doghouse for Nikki to help shield the canine from the frigid Iowa winters.

Leaning back gripping the leather leash for dear life, this wannabe sled dog used me as fodder for workouts on the hilly roads of the neighborhood. I slipped and tripped on winter-iced roads, fresh from a January blizzard. Anyone observing this spectacle would have thought the dog had taken me prisoner and was dragging me off to the guillotine. But I dared not let go. Tied up by a chain in the side yard and neglected, Nikki escaped more than once. He'd break the chain or pull his tether's anchor tie straight out of the ground, then charge through the neighborhood and nearby no-till cornfields with rapturous abandon. "Nikki! Nikki! Here Nikki!" I'd yell through the tears stinging my face in the subzero gales. I was exhausted. Exhausted trying to take care of this dog. Exhausted trying to take care of myself. But I didn't take care of either well. Somehow, I just didn't have the capacity. Not having really experienced how it felt, I didn't know how to take care of myself. I only knew how to reflect or gauge what other peoples' emotions and reactions were, not my own.

That day in the field, searching for that wild canine, epitomizes my childhood loneliness and abandonment. I didn't care, and didn't want to care, about anything. After Nikki escaped one morning and terrorized one of Jamie's sheep to death, Dad had no choice but to give Nikki away, ostensibly to a farmer with fenced land where he could run free. I'm not convinced he didn't actually head off to the Rainbow Bridge.

In school as well as at home, I did what the teachers said and didn't get into trouble. I acquiesced to the path of least resistance and followed rules for the sake of following rules. All my scrapbook-bound report cards showed me as a good student, conscientious and diligent. The good girl, never rocking the boat, I did what I had to get along with everyone. I had learned this would get me feelings of acceptance and help me avoid the shame of disapproval. It became my way of fitting in to the world around me.

JENNY

"Grief is extremely powerful. It's easy to get stuck in your pain and remain bitter, angry, or depressed. Grief grabs your heart and doesn't seem to let go."
—DAVID KESSLER, *FINDING MEANING*

Jenny became my fifth sister, born as an "oops" to Mom and Dad when I was in second grade. I sometimes wondered—with five children averaging sixteen months apart—if Mom knew where babies came from, and I always assumed she had "figured it out" after Kelly's birth five years prior. But they were Catholic after all, which banned "artificial" means of birth control.

One late winter afternoon, Mom, standing at the stove stirring up supper, unconsciously set her Kool in the crook of the red plastic ashtray after a long drag. Dad walked in through the dark, narrow hallway door from the garage. "How are things?" he said with a rumple in his furry mono-brow.

"I'm pregnant." Mom said wearily with resignation.

"Well, we'll have to deal with it," he said.

Twelve-year-old Colleen, sitting on the family room floor and thumbing through a Donny Osmond-cover *Teen* magazine, heard the whole exchange. She glanced up, rolled her eyes, and started crying, her long brown hair falling across her down-turned face. As an adult, Colleen recalled being embarrassed and self-conscious about her family of "five girls, no boys" and just trying to fit in at her new junior high school. None of her friends' parents were having babies, and just like any American teenager—making friends her focus—she didn't want to stand out. She was breaking away from family and starting to become her own person. She felt overwhelmed, awkward and alone about the situation. Later as an adult she stated: "I think right away I knew that I wouldn't get any help from Mom and Dad on how to navigate this with the world or my friends. I didn't feel like I would get less of their attention. I think I was used to that and okay with it." Feeling a bit betrayed by her parents, Colleen started rejecting herself as a good student. She admitted she started ignoring her schoolwork and hanging around older kids in the neighborhood and school—kids who "partied" or who neglected homework.

Later at supper, Mom announced pragmatically, "Girls, I'm pregnant. I'm going to have a baby." Dad stayed silent chewing his supper with elbows on the table, staring at the nightly news droning on in the background behind us. Jill, Kelly, and I perked up and took on Mom's scant enthusiasm for having a baby in the house, imagining the cuddling, cooing, and happiness a newborn surely brought to our somber normal. Rhonda sat silent, looking at Colleen.

"Ooh! A baby!" I said excitedly, looking at Kelly with a grin.

"I hope it's a boy," Jill said with optimism. Colleen just looked down at her plate with her eyes closed, shaking her head. I instantly relaxed my enthusiasm, automatically taking the lead from my eldest sister, warranted, intentional or not.

Jenny became an infusion of delight to our household, cute and affable, a welcome distraction to the melancholy climate permeating the walls in which we lived. We'd sit around her lying on one of the embroidered quilts Grandma made especially for her and spread out on the family room floor trying to make her laugh. Mom showed us how to hold her newborn head up because the muscles weren't yet developed, and we learned how to fold and change a cloth diaper, careful not to stick Jenny with the oversized safety pins. Mom breast fed for a while, but also made bottles of whole milk and dark Karo syrup for when she and Dad were out at night.

Dad became a blubbering, goofy mess when talking and playing with Jenny. Rocking gently in his La-Z-Boy, Jenny cradled in his arm, he'd look up at the ceiling then bring his face down to the side of her cheek and neck, blowing raspberries into her supple flesh. Jenny, in her blue puppy-print-footed pajamas and Iowa State University stocking cap, would belly laugh so hard she could barely catch her breath. "I'm gonna getcha! Here I come!" he'd tease. Similar to later years when doting on grandchildren, I'd never seen him so happy as when holding her, her worshiping gaze completely focused on him and his antics.

Although Mom didn't have the *What to Expect* book series as I did to help her through pregnancy and the first years of a baby's life, Mom was obviously experienced in raising a baby and the natural progression of rolling over, sitting up, and walking babies take. One day, Kelly was sitting beside Jenny on another family-created blanket jingling the red Fisher-Price Happy Apple toy trying to make her smile.

She looked up and saw Mom's concerned expression as she worked to get Jenny to sit up by herself. But Jenny's muscles imitated jelly, and she just slumped over in a heap. Soon after, doctors diagnosed her with cerebral palsy. I remember accompanying Mom to the thrice-weekly physical therapy sessions, learning how to move and "exercise" Jenny's legs and arms in an effort to induce them into working more independently.

Preteen Colleen and the rest of us were left in charge of Jenny's care—and each other—when Mom and Dad were out at Vic's some nights. Although easygoing and good-natured most of the time, Jenny had inconsolable bouts of crying no one—not even Dad—could manage. One night at his wit's end, Dad—walking the darkened living room floor, bouncing her on his shoulder—spanked Jenny, hard, on her diapered butt. We were all spanked when we misbehaved—part of the "spanked generation," I guess—rarely with the palm of a hand but with a wooden yardstick. We used to line up, one behind the other when Mom had had enough of our bickering—or whatever perturbation she couldn't deal with—and take our hits, sometimes breaking the implement in half. None of us sustained physical marks after such a thrashing but learned our place in this authoritarian-style discipline pretty quickly. The spankings didn't quell Jenny's cries and never did.

On one of those nights, I remember taking care of Jenny. Mom and Dad were at Vic's, and Colleen and Rhonda were out in the neighborhood with friends. Jill and Kelly were watching TV in the family room. I held Jenny as she cried, noticing her tear-soaked eye patch meant to develop the muscle in the lazy organ. Alone in the dim living room, I rocked her back and forth in the dark, walnut stained,

US-bicentennial chair. I shifted her in my arms to try and console her. She arched her spine, and I put her on my shoulder. I patted her back, but nothing would soothe her. Out of frustration and impatience, I spanked Jenny's butt, shame overcoming me. I emulated my father, the only response I could come up with in my ten-year-old brain. She only wailed harder, gasping for breath between sobs. When Colleen walked through the back door and saw us, she grimaced and shook her head. "I don't know what to do. She just won't stop," I told her, close to tears myself.

Colleen called Mom and Dad at Vic's, begging them to come home. "Jenny won't stop crying," she pleaded. I still feel guilty about that night.

At nearly two years old, doctors diagnosed Jenny with cancer, and she had to have one lung removed from her tiny body in an attempt to halt the aggressive disease. The next several weeks are a blur to me, but I recall how quiet the house was while Jenny, Mom, and Dad were at the hospital. Much too soon after the brutal surgery, we learned the cancer had spread. In my memory this time seems to have dragged on for months, but in recalling events with my sisters and aunts today, only a few weeks of time had passed, mercifully fast.

Mom and Dad had an unimaginable decision to make: continue to remove tumors and baneful body parts in hopes of eventually arresting the cancer's progression or have mercy on their baby daughter's little body and let nature take its course. They chose the latter. Jenny died early one morning in the hospital less than six weeks after her two-year birthday party, neither Mom nor Dad there to say their goodbyes. After the call from the hospital, Mom quietly came into each of our bedrooms, touched our backs and gently said, "No school today, hun. Jenny died last night." She lingered there a few minutes stroking the hair out of my face. I remember this as one of the only times Mom's tender touch and soothing voice comforted me.

The days following were a blur with Grandma and aunts coming in and out of the house to support and console. Somehow funeral arrangements were made, a notice in the paper written and filed and baby books completed with photos celebrating a life cut short. I can't say who made all those decisions back then. The motto of this mid-western family could have been "buck it up." Dad silently sobbed while standing, looking out the front door's small, twelve-inch, square window. Everyone else pretended not to see, keeping busy with whatever preoccupation could allow them to avoid stepping into the foreign world of empathic conversation. Hard to find among the family, the expression of emotion seemed almost shameful.

In a recent discussion with my aunt, she recalled remembering standing in the kitchen with Mom soon after Jenny died. "It was very difficult to talk to Mary. She didn't want to talk about it. She didn't want to share what she was experiencing at all," she recollected. She wanted to help but wasn't allowed in. She couldn't relate to Mom at all. "You could see her suffering, but I didn't feel like I was reaching her at all. I remember thinking of her family. She doesn't have anybody for her."

Like every other Catholic death I've experienced, a wake took place the day prior to the actual funeral service, with visitation for friends and family to share condolences and sit quietly in rows facing the open casket. For some fiendish reason, Jenny's wake spanned two tortuous days, complete with candles, flowers, organ music, and agonizingly strained smiles shared in upturned, exhausted faces to tongue-tied strangers. Unlike at my friend George's funeral, Jenny appeared in plain view, a presence begging for attention but emanating an energy of mystery and discretion. I wanted to go near and kneel beside her, feel her presence, and understand what was happening. Grandma encouraged me to come nearer, putting her arm around my shoulder and leading me closer. I did until the discomfort made it too unbearable. Kelly touched Jenny's cheek and Grandma bent over the casket to give the lifeless body one final kiss, almost collapsing the whole display before the grievous event finally ended. My uncle grabbed her arm and held her back.

I've always acknowledged I've not been subject to any capital "T" trauma in my life—never sexually or physically abused, raped, or beaten. But if carrying your deceased baby sister down the aisle at her funeral isn't traumatic, then I don't know what is. The century old, historic Catholic church reverberated with organ music as we waited in the dark vestibule. My sisters and I numbly looked around at each other as unfamiliar adults placed us in order around the casket—Kelly and I in front—and showed us how to grip the handles firmly. Family and friends packed the sanctuary to the stained glass, Way of the Cross windows. Tears and snot streaming down my face, people's pitiful faces following us to the altar, I couldn't spare a hand to grab the tissue Grandma had put in my sleeve to wipe the decency back on it. I was a cat in a shower; I wanted to run for my life.

I don't remember what happened right after Jenny's funeral, but a luncheon probably ensued in the low-ceiling church basement with food and "fellowship" with people who somehow missed the forty-eight-hour vigil prior. Things at home quickly returned to "normal"—neither Mom nor

Dad spoke to us about what happened or how we were feeling or considered therapy for us or them. Jenny's things were packed up and put away. I'm not sure if it was the time period, the generation we lived in, or simply the "just move on" family stoicism, but we didn't acknowledge the pain we were all in, the impact of losing a beloved family member. We just continued as if nothing happened.

Thirty years later, my sister Jill faced a similar tragedy when her six-month old daughter, Isabella, died from streptococcus pneumonia. Jill and her husband, however, received counseling to learn how to deal with the unfathomable loss. "You feel cold after the death of a child, changed," she remembered. "You have a new normal. You don't want to do the same things you did before. You don't want to be around the same people, maybe because you can't handle the sympathy, the uncomfortable glances, the burden of exposing those feelings once again or explaining the difficulties of every day." Jill and her husband were changed, as were our parents.

Even before Jenny died, I rarely saw Mom and Dad talk about anything remotely dealing with feelings or emotion, and the death of a daughter could not break them out of the trappings of their personal hell. In the years after Jenny, the previously meager outward affection between them suffered even more. Exploring their pain and leaning on each other for comfort somehow seemed off limits in their relationship and only appeared to grow exponentially larger after her death. The pats on the ass stopped, and only terse sentences passed between them. For doctrinal reasons, divorce could not be considered as an opportunity to ease the psychological weight on their hearts.

Mom and Dad's social life also waned after Jenny died. They lost touch with what friends they had and went out to

Vic's much less frequently. They were now "the couple who lost a child," an unbearable discomfort.

Right before Jenny's funeral, Dad hugged Colleen and told her he loved her for the first time she could remember. None of us could remember seeing him cry before then. Dad seemed to loosen up after Jenny passed. Stern and unapologetic before, his heart seemed to have softened, and he raised his voice less often if we irritated him in any way. Maybe distracted with grief, a piece of his heart had faded away with Jenny. Dad severely limited his smoking to one or two cigarettes a day, even discarding the pedestal ashtray furniture fixture next to his family room lounge chair. Though warnings on cigarette packages cautioning users of the dangers of smoking to fetuses wouldn't become required until several years later, I wonder if Dad (and Mom) felt responsible for Jenny's cancer.

Years later, Mom confessed to Colleen she never felt comforted by Dad after Jenny died and seemed bitter about it for years. "I was having a hard time, but he just couldn't comfort me. I don't think he had it in him," she said. Having lived with Mom's—and Dad's, for that matter—lack of outward emotion and empathy, I wonder if they were any consolation to each other at all.

After losing Jenny, Mom switched to reading romance novels, shutting herself in her bedroom for hours in the day as a means of escape. She soon sought part-time work, maybe as a way to keep herself busy. We were, after all, growing up and needing her less for daily life tasks. She rarely asked us about our day or what happened at school.

Although I didn't learn from home how to express my feelings, my teacher at school, Mrs. Tansey, helped me recognize my emotions were valid, that everyone had them, and that they were normal and okay. She came to Jenny's funeral, and, in hindsight, I recognize her as a lifeline, probably saving me from a descent into acting out. She walked me into the gymnasium at school the day I returned after Jenny's death and funeral. Presidential elections were coming up and students were holding a "rally," carrying signs for either Carter or Ford. I really didn't know what was going on, but Mrs. Tansey, with her arm around me and gentle manner, walked me over to the circle and inserted me in with the other students. I remember her standing there watching as we marched.

I became more of a "good girl," trying even harder to make my parents happy. My sisters have their own stories about what Jenny's death meant to them and how it shaped them, but according to the 2003 book *When Children Die: Improving Palliative and End-of-Life Care for Children and Their Families*, the death of a child has profound effects on the parent-child relationship: "Adolescents are more vulnerable to depression in response to the parents' grief and subsequent withdrawal from them as the adolescent goes through normal separation from the family." And "Siblings of children who die have also been found to be at greater risk for externalizing and internalizing problems ... within two years of the death." We all reacted and coped in our own way, but not entirely without each other to hold on to.

IGUANA

"Parents are the founders and CEOs of the family life that con-stitutes a child's world ... and parents remain shadow fig-ures in their children's lives and relationships—especially the children's relationships with one another—long after they are children no more."
—DEBORAH TANNEN, *YOU WERE ALWAYS MOM'S FAVORITE!*

One time, when my husband and I were watching old home movies of my sisters and I as young girls running around the house and backyard, he commented, "You guys aren't touch-ing or tussling with each other. You're all like singular robots playing for an audience. Where's the laughter and joy?" He was right. As much as I can't remember hugs or loving feel-ings from Mom and Dad, I also can't recall them coming from my sisters, either. I think when I left home—when we all left home—we were running away *from* something, just as much as *to* something.

Despite having grown up with the same parents our whole lives, and living in the same household, my sisters and I have always been separate and unique individuals. I never had the nature vs. nurture debate in my head. I remember my aunt saying more than once, "I will never understand how close in age you all are, grew up in the same household, but how very different you all are from one another." We all experienced the same parents, had the same resources growing up, and we all lost a baby sister, but we are all doing different things with our lives. We went our separate ways after high school and today live in five different states. Sure, we had some camaraderie, game playing, togetherness inevitable from living in the same household as we grew up, but I always felt something lacking in how we connected then and how we connect now.

"Iguana" materialized one afternoon as my sisters and I lounged around the family room watching reruns. Saying silly-sounding words to each other, we kept saying, "Iguana" over and over again, giggling and trying to find rhyming words as we protruded our lip out pronouncing the "gwah" sound. Somehow *Iguana* became the word we said when someone forgot something, spilled something, or made Mom or Dad mad. Did the dishwasher not get emptied? "Iguana did it." Did someone spill a drink on the counter? "It was Iguana." It became a "thing" from one of the few times I remember us as teenagers sitting around laughing and joking with each other. We call each other The Iguana Sisters to this day.

As teenagers we'd lounge around lazily in the family room trying not to annoy one another. Flopped on Dad's brown La-Z-Boy, her skinny legs draped over one arm, Kelly barked, "Move your head, Jill. I can't see." Jill had just thrown a sofa pillow on the floor in front of the TV and propped her elbow on it to hold her head up. The familiar theme song to *Gilligan's Island* sounded in the background, one we knew by heart and would frequently sing along to. Outstretched on the couch with her knees bent, Colleen flipped through a magazine and sighed. Rhonda sat in a side chair, knees up to her chest, biting her lip and twirling her long brown hair between her thumb and two fingers. I sat at a kitchen table chair turned to watch the screen, eating a saltine cracker.

Jill would be in the kitchen these days, always cooking up something. She'd stand at the stove, black plastic spatula in her hand, and one of us would yell, "Jill! Turn on the fan!" after the odor of fried egg permeated into the family room. Jill would delight us by figuring out how to make doughnuts in the FryDaddy sitting on the counter with God-knows-how-old grease inside. Sitting together at the supper table one night playing cards when Mom and Dad were out at Vic's, Colleen stuck her tongue out and gagged, "It's floating in butter!" As I peered over the large popcorn bowl in front of us, I saw her disgust. Kernels were floating in the melted butter Jill had put on the snack.

"I know. Mmmm," she grinned, digging her fingers in the greasy mess to get some more. Of all my sisters, Jill—fifteen months my senior—seemed most like a mother figure to me. I remember her showing me how to curl my hair on the first day of high school, helping me figure out what to wear on my first real date, and proudly calling me out as her "little sister" at school.

Afternoon snacking for us teens became a desperate and pointless endeavor. Although completely false in our household, we honestly expressed the "There's nothing to eat" dictum of the all-American teenager. We knew Mom, away at her new job at Powers Manufacturing Company sewing athletic wear, bought Doritos, marshmallow cookies, and shoestring potatoes at the local Hy-Vee supermarket. We just had to find them. So she had one iota of a chance to snack on them when she got home, Mom often hid them from us. Jill would rifle through each cupboard and drawer in the kitchen. "Did you look in the entryway cabinet? I'd say, as Jill grabbed a chair. The cabinets spanned clear to the ceiling and Jill put one foot on the chair and stood on the counter to reach the topmost door. She'd stand there on her tiptoes rummaging around seldom used bowls and pitchers.

"I found 'em!" she called in triumph, pushing a dusty vase aside and pulling the bag of Nacho Cheese Doritos out and handing it down to Rhonda.

"Don't eat them all!" I admonished.

We fought among ourselves to make sure we didn't eat the entire bag. We failed most of the time and cowered from the tongue lashing we'd get when Mom got home. As peacemaker of the house, I cringed when I saw only a few chips were in the bottom of the bag. I knew Mom would be pissed at not getting her snack. The house would also be in disarray from five bored, adolescent girls running in and out, leaving magazines, games, and curling irons strewn around in odd places in the house, and lunch dishes still in the sink and on counters. On more than one occasion I'd nag them to help me clean up, but—more often than not—it didn't get done in time. Mom would come home, slam her purse and keys on the kitchen counter when she saw our butts glued to our TV-watching perches. She'd sigh in disgust and say, "Girls! Did you do anything today?" We'd look around sheepishly at one another, not answering her. "I'm going to run away from home," she'd declare, stomping off down the hall to her bedroom, slamming the door behind her, supper preparation looming in front of her.

We shared other moments of connectedness and memories with reminiscence even today. With three finished bedrooms in the house, at some point in our cohabitation I shared a space with each of my sisters except Colleen. Colleen, being the eldest, got the pick of rooms and chose the room off the kitchen away from the others, and eventually set up a bedroom in the basement.

When Rhonda and I shared a room, we used to prop up on our elbows in the full-size bed, holding the covers over our heads like a makeshift tent. At night, we played Tiddlywinks beneath the canopy with a flashlight, talking and laughing until Mom knocked on our door to shush us up. Her reprimand usually didn't work, and we'd continue to play, lowering our voices to bare whispers. This I remember as one of the few times I played with Rhonda one-on-one. She was three years older than me and closer in age to Colleen, so we were in different junior high and high schools. I perceived Rhonda had a more difficult time dealing with Mom and Dad and following house rules growing up. She graduated early from high school and, at seventeen, left home, driving to Texas to look for work.

I loved games, puzzles, cards, and board games. While the wind howled outside during a blizzard, Mom would get us started on a 2,000-piece jigsaw puzzle in the dining room, and we'd all take our turns working the different angles, colors, and edge pieces until finished. During these snow days off school, I would challenge Kelly to a game fest. "Let's play every game in the house and keep a tally of who wins." She reluctantly agreed but quit after I beat her at *Go to the Head of the Class*, *Operation*, and then *Cribbage*. I couldn't get any of the others to play with me. Kelly confessed with pride much later she cheated a lot. My naive self never noticed. Of all my sisters, being just fifteen months younger than me, Kelly was my go-to playmate. Mom and Dad called her "The

Grub" because she always came in from playing outside with dirt under her fingernails and coating her ankles and neck. Always independent and outwardly confident, people used to think she preceded me in age.

As a little girl, and when I used to stay over at Grandma's house about fifteen minutes south of us in La Porte City, I could hear the nearby train horn and subsequent rattle of the wheels on the tracks. This and the steady neon-lit sign blinking "Vacancy" through the window from the hotel directly behind the house somehow comforted me. Grandma's house had a kind of hum, maybe because of the way she kept it, the purpose she brought to things she did both mundane and consequential. Grandma parented and "grandma-ed" with an authoritarian style and, although we feared and shunned her command, Grandma seemed to know her place in the world and had direction in her life. She had an air of confidence in her beliefs about the world aligned with her strict Catholic faith, how to keep a house, or how to raise a child. Her self-confidence and air of purposefulness comforted me back then. Today I can often hear a nearby train horn at night as I turn off my grown-up bedside lamp. It brings me a warm sense of peace and nostalgia.

I struggle to find a similar feeling of warmth and content in memories of living in my parents' home as a schoolgirl and into my teenage years. I know my sisters were connective tissue throughout my growing up, as most siblings are, I guess, and we laugh about plenty of connecting points today. However, we didn't connect in so many ways, too.

A close friend of mine who grew up with just one brother has on more than one occasion expressed her long-felt desire to have a sister. I just look at her in bewilderment. I don't regret having sisters, but I didn't, for too long a time, really think I "needed" them nor did I think they ever played that big of a part in my life. *Sisters? Meh. Who needs 'em?* I generally believed.

Like keeping the house clean for Mom, I also needed to keep a sense of peace and order when parties were held at our house by both my parents and siblings alike. When we first moved out to East Shaulis Road, Mom and Dad held occasional evening card parties at the house. Sitting on Dad's lap in my pajamas, I'd take a swig of his Budweiser as the adults, cards in hand, cigarettes hanging from their grinning lips, tipped their heads back and laughed. Dad bounced me on his thigh and said, "That's enough, now. Time to go to bed." I headed to bed but lay wide eyed on my back, covers up to my chin, stiff as a board until all the guests left and the house became quiet again. I felt vulnerable and unsafe on these nights. In the morning I'd help pick up empty beer cans strewn around the house.

I felt similarly, but more responsible, when Colleen and Rhonda held the few high school keg parties at our house while Mom and Dad traveled out of town for the occasional long weekend getaway with friends. Apparently, at ages eleven to seventeen we were deemed responsible enough that Grandma didn't get asked to stay overnight with us. With a pit in my stomach, I'd nervously hide in my back bedroom through the ruckus, Gene Simmons and Kiss blaring from someone's car stereo, people yelling and running around and through the house, doors slamming, inexperienced drinkers puking in the bathroom next door to my room. I'd peek out down the long hallway several times during the night until silence at three o'clock in the morning gave me the courage to walk out onto the sticky floors and check out the damage. Every light on in the house, I'd check to make sure my older sisters were still breathing, flicked the light switches and locked the doors.

One early morning, like a scene from *Risky Business*, kids were still there at seven o'clock in the morning, and I started cleaning because Mom and Dad were due home in just a few hours. The actual party didn't upset me so much—drunken teenagers driving away from our house back to town a few miles away in the middle of the night aside—but the thought of my parents' impending rage and disappointment motivated me to make everything seem okay and normal. Although I didn't invite a person to the parties, I felt solely responsible for ensuring everything got put back in place, nobody got mad, nobody yelled. Somehow my isolation and feeling of separateness were magnified when routines, norms, and rules were not followed.

When each of my sisters and I turned forty, we joined the birthday girl in or near her hometown to celebrate. We had a spa weekend at Colleen's during a Wisconsin snowstorm, made a true getaway in St. John Island when Rhonda lived there, did Christmas shopping in New York City for Jill's, spent mine at a friend's condo in Palm Coast, Florida, and went on an Iowa wine tour at Kelly's. These events included Mom. The first day or so were light and fun, but each ended with someone screaming at someone else and one or more of us crying. I half laugh with friends that my sisters and I can stand only about forty-eight hours with one another before someone gets the knives out.

It seems to me we can touch base, get an update on each other's lives, reminisce a bit about our shared past, but can't seem to go any deeper. Things get tense, and some kind of inner distrust persists between one another. The safe space we long to find never appears. Like an invisible force field, we bounce off it in frustration, fighting back at each other not realizing something within our own selves is holding us back, not each other. We weren't taught how to care. We weren't taught how to hold another's vulnerability as sacred gifts. We weren't taught how to nurture each other. We didn't see how to connect with one another on any level other than superficially. We've all had to navigate our own experience with CEN. Each of us have had to learn how to take care of ourselves, show our emotions. We didn't see parents model those behaviors, so we all had to develop these skills on our own.

In the *New York Times Magazine* 2014 article "Forty Portraits in Forty Years" about the Brown sisters' series of portraits displayed at the Museum of Modern Art, author Susan Minot acknowledges viewers are not privy to the inner lives or true relationship between the sisters:

"It is the endurance of sisterhood in particular. With each passing year, the sisters seem to present more of a united front. Earlier assertions of their individuality—the arms folded across the chest, the standing apart—give way to a literal leaning on one another, as if independence is no longer such a concern."

I want to think my sisters and I are headed in that direction—less independence, more leaning on each other. Like the home movies my husband observed, I've compared images of us in our younger years. In one it looks as if we are ready for church, sitting side by side on the saggy cushions of a gold and green flowered sofa—Rhonda sullen and pouting, me in my too-big dress and dirty saddle shoes faking a smile, Colleen in her lavender suit and long dark hair facing forward with a faraway look, Kelly sitting at attention looking down, and Jill, red-faced as if she'd just been crying. We were touching each other but just enough to make it into the picture shot. In another photo from my daughter's wedding a few years ago, we were all smiling. Kelly is leaning forward into my back, and I'm leaning back into her. Jill is leaning back with turned head into Rhonda who is looking up as if laughing. Colleen is on the end next to Rhonda looking over at all of us.

The bond of shared childhood and shared experiences can never be taken away from my sisters and me. Maybe I'm making too little of this fact. I think being a middle child and having sisters around, experiencing the same home life, the same parenting, the same dysfunction helped me cope, a kind of connective tissue I could flow along with and follow until I could run away from home myself.

ADRIFT

"A rat in a maze is free to go anywhere, as long as it stays inside the maze."

—MARGARET ATWOOD, *A HANDMAID'S TALE*

I will never understand why my neighbor's daughter and a friend's son didn't get their learners' driving permits the minute they turned fifteen. It didn't make sense to me, the acquaintance's son who, after graduating high school top of his class and ready for college, took a semester and just hung out at home with his parents. I craved my independence, freedom. All my sisters and I left home upon graduating, not wasting a second of finding our way in the world or escaping the black hole sucking the life out of us there. Colleen enrolled in a finishing school in Wisconsin. Rhonda graduated a semester early and fled to Texas to work. Jill entered a local university and walked on to the volleyball team. Kelly tried her hand at a couple of local schools, then moved to Des Moines for work and another community college. I enrolled at Iowa State University (ISU), initially in the architecture program. After switching majors each semester for the first couple of years, I got to know my advisor well.

Not having a sense of who I was or wanted to be, I took direction from anyone who would dole it out. I had no idea what I wanted to do with my life and no idea how to find out. I didn't even know to ask. I only knew what other people told me I should do or excelled at. Jonice Webb in a 2018 website article describes how CEN contributes to this inner confusion:

"A funny thing happens when you are not connected with your feelings: you don't get to make major life decisions based on your feelings. And, after all, our feelings are our most effective guides to our true selves. This is why so many people who grew up with Childhood Emotional Neglect end up in jobs, marriages, and locations that are not quite right for them. Going through the motions, living the life that chose you instead of the life you chose to live, you may find yourself feeling off-kilter, unfulfilled, and somewhat at-sea in your adult life. This lowers your defenses to depression."

A good student (conscientious and diligent, remember?), I graduated among the top ten of my class of more than four-hundred students, only one B+ standing in my way of high school academic perfection. According to the messages I received from teachers and counselors, I should be an engineer, a doctor, an architect, something to utilize those skills and make the gender proud. I did love math which came easy for me; I saw it as a game, a puzzle of fun, and the first homework done at school-day end.

Decades later when my own kids came home from school I'd eagerly ask, "Got any math homework to do today?" A carny, eyes wide and crazed, I'd motion them to the kitchen counter, "Sit right up here. That's right kids. Come see the show of your lives! Gather 'round. Lay out your addition, sub-traction tables, your story problems, your linear equations. Keep your eyes wide open; you won't want to miss any of it!" The chess master of my kids' homework, I'd have them lay out their worksheets and textbooks in a line on the table for my monitoring pleasure. I even made my preteen son cry once. "But that's not the way we are supposed to do it, Mom!" he sobbed after I showed him a cool short cut for thinking about his fractions. Needless to say, none of my children excelled in or got excited by math or science.

One day as a high school sophomore, a guidance coun-selor suggested I complete a career direction survey. So elated to finally find out what I should be when I grew up, I took the hall pass she gave me and hustled to the library. Standing at the check-out counter, tapping my pencil eraser on my note-book, I excitedly grabbed the decision-tree-like quiz from the librarian. The series of cards which made up the pre-com-puter-era questionnaire was similar to the card-catalogue system used to organize and index the collection's materi-als. Reading each card's questions—"Which of the following activities do you prefer to engage in your spare time?"—I'd stick my No. 4 in the hole at the top of the card matching my preference, pulling out those careers not suiting my passion and aptitude. I then moved to the next question—"Which of the following activities most interests you?" Holding my breath as I came to the final thin batch of careers meant just for me, I came to the final question and inserted my pencil in the hole. Feelings of disappointment and distrust came over me after reading the card. According to psychologists, my ideal career was—drum roll, please—pest control technician.

Though I'm sure an amiable profession, I did not become—or even explore the possibilities of becoming—a pest control technician. I did, however, eventually marry a man with a minor in entomology, so maybe there was something to the test, albeit subliminally. I moved on to reading my first (but not last) career advice book, *What Color Is Your Parachute?*, ending up more confused than ever about which direction my life should take.

I did what everyone seemed to be telling me back then, "You need to go to college." The school guidance counselor looked at my grades and said, "You should go to college." My drafting teacher and track coach, whom I trusted as a sort of confidant, said, "Go to college." All my friends were going to and talking about the college they were planning to attend. "What college are you going to?" they'd ask to my bewildered expression. Every person I asked for advice said the same thing, three little words, "Go to college." My fate was sealed.

Everyone directed me to what I excelled at, but I don't remember anyone asking me what I wanted to do. Not that I knew myself. I had perfected the "do-what-you're-told-so-no-one-gets-mad" motto for living. If everyone else approved, or everyone else told me to do something, it must be the path for me. In college, after volunteering with children at The Arc of Alachua County, a nonprofit serving people with developmental disabilities, I considered being a physical therapist. When my kids were in middle school, I applied for a middle school math teacher position, actually submitting my paperwork to the district. I played Whac-A-Mole with my future—no points scored.

The first visit to my advisor's office at ISU came swiftly freshman year after my first Physics 101 exam. Somehow, I had avoided taking physics in high school. Following my fellow students' sage advice—"You've got to see what Mr. Johnson did today in chemistry class!"—I opted into the quirky man's class rather than physics as my science credit. The three-hundred-student college class and the seemingly untouchable professor and eventual graduate student teaching the basic class overwhelmed me, and I bailed after a few weeks. I changed my major to landscape architecture (LA), which didn't have a science requirement at the time.

In high school I had taken two drafting classes. In the age before computers, we sat on stools at large, mint-green drafting tables outfitted with pencil tray, T-square and forty-five-degree triangle. I loved the precision of drawing lines with a straightedge and creating perfectly parallel lines, removing any mistakes with an erasing shield. This imitated coloring down in my grandmother's basement. Forget the design part—drawing a structure to accommodate human needs and making it safe to inhabit—I just wanted to draw straight lines with a straightedge and look at beautiful homes, especially the ones with mansard-style roofs.

So, when I checked "famous architect" off the list of possible careers, I had to pivot to something, some other major, some other direction so I could continue to fulfill my dad's expectation and pride at me attending a major state university. Sitting on the front stoop of the East Shaulis Road house as a teenager, I remember looking across the road at the rows of corn waving to and fro in unison as if dancing to a swoony song in the warm summer breeze. I smelled the faint scent of fresh cut grass mixed with a waft of my friend's pig farm down the road and listened to the birds chirping and flitting at the feeder in front of the family room window. I wanted this feeling to last forever. I may not have known much about what I wanted for myself, but I vowed then to go outside to experience nature each day of the rest of my life. Remembering this, landscape architecture seemed the perfect career path.

According to a 2013 Federal Reserve Bank of New York study, only 27 percent of college graduates are working in their majors (Pulmer, 2013). Apparently, the experience of college (forget the millions of dollars invested in and collected by the university system over the decades) is what matters to employers and what makes the difference in students' lives and not the actual degree. A 2015 survey by Hart Research Associates showed nearly 91 percent of employers believe an employee's critical thinking and problem-solving skills are more important than their college major. Knowing this now relieves some guilt, anguish, and societal pressure from me when I think of my zigzagging and haphazard educational path and subsequent "career" choices (if you can call it that). I did learn a lot in college, a lot about myself and the big, wide world—things I never would have extracted from life on East Shaulis Road.

At college I utilized the independence skills I learned from home and made friends and had fun. I came in as a freshman with a high school boyfriend, and although it took me two years to definitively break it off with him, I learned how to stand up for myself in relationships and listen to my inner feeling of "this is not right." It opened something in me and made me stronger. But it was ugly. Similar to the nightcrawler I used to coax out of the sprinkler-soaked ground before summer family fishing trips, I was pulled out of my comfort zone, and something kept trying to suck me back in. I didn't know what was pulling me out, but I knew if stayed in the ground I would have suffocated. Eventually, I broke the relationship off. I knew I had made the right decision, based on my feelings, whether I could express it or not. I rarely again hesitated telling men in my life what I wanted. It felt like a breakthrough.

After flip-flopping declared majors a few more times, landscape architecture stuck, and I received a degree with honors after five years of all-night studios, experiential on-site classes, and education in land ethics. This fulfilled my yearning for closeness to the land and natural environment. But after five years, I still couldn't picture myself working in the LA field. I had rumblings LA wasn't good enough and that I could and should do more. I decided I needed to go to graduate school. I feared actually entering the real world I sensed I had no business or passion stepping into. I still had no clue what I wanted to do with my life.

Coaxed by a couple of LA professors, I applied to graduate school in the LA department at Louisiana State University and learned of my acceptance right away with a graduate assistantship. This appealed to me on a couple levels. One, as a natural progression of my LA degree, I wouldn't have "wasted" those previous five years of schooling. Two, they wanted me, and my ISU professors were pointing me in that direction. But I still heard the nagging voice I should be more and somehow "owed" it to the world to prove myself.

At the time I applied to LSU, I also applied and was accepted to University of Florida's Coastal Engineering graduate program. Yes, engineering. In LA at ISU, as a key part of the sustainability curriculum, we learned about aeolian processes and how the "hills" of western Iowa were formed. Iowa is a vast grassland-turned-farmland, and mitigating the loss of valued topsoil is imperative. Accepted to UF thinking I could learn about shoreline sand dune formation and erosion somehow validated the voice in my head that I should prove myself, not to myself but to the outside world. *Everyone will respect me if I go into engineering,* the voice seduced. *You will finally be good enough,* it nagged. Although an inner voice this time, it did not come from me. It spoke from the past. The voice told me I had to live up to someone else's vision of who I was; I needed to utilize those natural IQ skills in math and show the world something. Today, I often remind myself, *Don't believe everything you think.* I wish I had that skill of introspection back then.

The spring of my final year at ISU, I nonchalantly opened the letter from LSU Department of Landscape Architecture.

Dear, Ms. Anderson,

We are pleased to offer you a graduate student position and assistantship in our department. However, we have not heard from you regarding your acceptance of this offer. Please respond to us by March 15 so we know to hold the position for you or offer it to another student. We look forward to hearing from you soon.

I quickly scanned the note and dropped it on the table without another thought. The next week during spring break, I headed to Florida to check out Gainesville and meet the professors in the engineering department at UF. I would confirm my decision for graduate school after the visit. But I didn't really give the offer any real thought. A blinder inside my head wouldn't let me see the possibilities there and held me back from considering this option and exploring what I wanted for my future. Certainly flattered they wanted me, I didn't consider going there to meet the professors. The pull to prove myself in engineering proved too great. After the Florida visit, I wrote a one-sentence letter to LSU telling them I would not become a Tiger.

The summer after I graduated from ISU, I married the entomology minor. Bryce, a graduate student in LA at the time, also grew up in Waterloo. A few years older than me, he attended high school with my sisters Colleen and Rhonda. I graduated with his younger brother, so we had some connections in the town. We planned for Bryce to complete his graduate project from whatever town we landed in, whether Gainesville or Baton Rouge. When I committed to UF, Bryce looked for a job in the college town, but our five-year plan included heading to southwest Florida after I graduated.

I loved the challenging differential equations classes and somehow made it through three physics courses at UF, narrowly eking out a "C" in accompanying labs. I loved the theoretical nature of the lectures and readings (give me Einstein and quantum physics theory any day) but don't try to get me to think about this in any practical way. I loved school, wishing for a career as a life-long student, but it took me no closer to discovering my own identity and passion. Pretty quickly I found myself on the wrong path once again.

One Saturday afternoon in my second year at UF, Bryce walked in the front door of the fourplex to me crying at the kitchen table. Pencil in hand, notebook, grid paper, and three different physics calculus and differential equations textbooks open in front of me, I sat hunched over, both elbows on the table, sobbing. "I don't think I can do this."

He cocked his head and looked at the hieroglyphics on the pages in front of me. "Yeah. I don't know how you are doing it, either, Boo. This stuff is insane."

"Not this," I sniffed, nodding to the problems in front of me. "This is great. I *love* this." Bryce wrinkled his brow and widened his eyes.

"I don't want to be an engineer. I don't know what I am doing here." I said shaking my head.

Bryce later confided to me about the alarm bells going off inside him that day. He also knew something was wrong but didn't know what to think or do about it.

So proceeded my three and a half years at UF. Mostly I played my "conscientious and diligent" student part well and tried not to think about feeling out of place or what I would do after graduating. Checking an engineering degree off the list left me completely void and empty. A rat new to the laboratory environment and rules, I had entered the life maze and took all the wrong turns, ending up in a windowless corner with no other door to go through or path to follow. And it seemed someone had just turned off the light.

THE BLACK DOG

—

"I am mentally ill. I can say that. I am not ashamed of that. I survived that. I'm still surviving it, but bring it on—better me than you."
—CARRIE FISHER, ABC NEWS PRIMETIME INTERVIEW

I don't know how long I had been sitting there—an hour? Two? The closed plastic mini-blinds obscured the barred front windows of the six-hundred-square-foot fourplex we rented and let only a filter of afternoon sunlight in. I sat cross-legged on the pink, saggy sofa, an acquisition from a graduating college roommate a couple years earlier in Ames, Iowa. We hauled the grungy piece twelve hundred miles in a small U-Haul truck to Gainesville. Along with it came a makeshift electric cable reel converted into a coffee table, a kitchen table bought from one of my husband's college fraternity buddies, and cinder blocks and a two-by-twelve TV stand. With my husband's $17,000-a-year salary, we lived as college students with the promise of my engineer's salary on the horizon—one I knew I couldn't keep.

Numb from head to toe, I stared at the dining table in the dusky room with Romeo, our black-and-tan German Shepherd, at my feet. Expected to graduate in a couple of months with a master's degree, I had no desire, excitement, aspiration for my future career. I had come to a dead end with absolutely no passion left inside me. Nobody was there showing me the next turn, offering any options, or asking what I wanted. I didn't have the skills or self-confidence to find those answers myself. I didn't even think I deserved the gratification for myself. Although I didn't identify it at the time, I was majorly depressed.

I continued through the motions, following the "rules" I learned, and headed to "step two" of making a life, just as my family and culture had taught: Step one—go to college. Step two—get a good job. It's all I knew to do. All I was told to do, searching for the steering wheel for my life but not finding the vehicle. I did graduate, and—after working temp jobs for a few months—landed a job at the Florida Department of Natural Resources (DNR) Bureau of Coastal Engineering in Tallahassee, 150 miles away. One of my graduate advisors from this department had let me know of the opening. My husband, Bryce, and I managed my weekly commute until a few months into the job. Our essentially nonexistent birth control methods succumbed to the release of financial pressure on us after I became gainfully employed, and I got pregnant.

After Haley was born, I worked part time from Gainesville for DNR for a year, plunging myself into baby rearing and motherhood. I loved being a mother, but the feelings coming up in me were antithetical to the women-can-do-anything-a-man-can-do-even-a-full-time-job-and-raising-children cultural message I grew up with and believed at the time. The feelings confused me. Societal pressure and self-imposed expectations meant I'd have a full-time career and drop my baby off at daycare five days a week. Another part wrestled with the drive to throw myself one hundred percent into caring for and raising this sponge of a human we'd brought into the world. Truly torn as surely thousands of women before me and since then, I faced a dilemma. Not prepared to make these decisions, I didn't even know how to think about making them. Thousands of miles away, my sisters and parents didn't talk about such things or open up enough to help me navigate.

On one hand I knew I needed to contribute to the household income and certainly validate my standing as a graduate degree-holding woman in the workforce. On the other, the instinctive and innate desire to nurture and develop my child was strong in me. Still staring at the blank wall of my career path, I opted to focus on raising children and continued part time at DNR for a year. Then I worked part-time jobs around Bryce's schedule, just to make ends meet. This limited the care-giving needs—outside the home at least—of our baby. I held on to same-age-as-me supermodel Cindy Crawford's quote about life, "You can have it all, just not all at the same time" (Quotefancy, 2022). I would focus on myself later; my child needed to come first at the moment. Right or wrong, with this as my excuse, I turned all my attention away from myself and my own personal growth and internal happiness.

Several months later, rumpled coverings from the previous night's sleep all around me, I lay in our queen-size bed in the master bedroom of our 1,100-square-foot home. We had moved into the house less than a month before Haley joined our family. Somehow, we managed to get the mortgage broker to believe I would remain gainfully employed for the next several years, and we were solvent enough to afford the payments. When we first stepped into the three-bedroom, two-bath "cottage," as Bryce called it, with its Pepto-Bismol pink walls and fenced backyard, we knew it fit into our absurdly optimistic five-year plan for our married life. So, we moved our made-for-college-student furniture in and dug into domestic life, ready or not.

Nearly a year later, I heard ten-month-old Haley stir in the small room across the hall but just kept staring at the ceiling, not able to move. It must have been close to noon—I wasn't quite sure—and I still had my nightgown on. The birds were chirping outside, but a silent pressure in the room surrounded me. An anvil, it weighed on me making me inapt to move. My limbs were frozen in place, disconnected from my mind. They seemed glued to the exhausted bed sheets, sucked by gravity into the spongy mattress. Acknowledging something was wrong with me and how I felt—or didn't feel—I began reading about depression and mood.

I had recently read an interview with actress Carrie Fisher about her depression and bipolar disease where she described the "black dog" hanging around her at all times, lurking in the background, ready to lunge at anything trying to work its way in to incite happiness or joy (ABC News, 2000). The term has also been attributed to Winston Churchill and even referenced as early as Egyptian times as an icon for mental illness and depression. That day, my black dog sat at the foot of my bed, stoically "protecting'" me, surrounding me, holding me there with its silent, powerful presence.

A couple weeks later I found myself holding a prescription for Prozac in a sterile, cramped, eight-by-eight office after completing a five-minute multiple-choice survey. The pasty, overweight psychiatrist scribbled something on his notepad and grunted, "You have low-grade depression. Take this prescription, and it should help." My jaw slackened in astonishment. This was mental health treatment? I didn't need his callous indifference and dismissal. I needed the direct opposite. I needed someone to talk me through this. I needed someone to listen to me and help me understand my feelings and why I felt this way and give me tools to manage.

I looked at the titles on the short bookshelf to his left. "What about therapy? Could I maybe talk with someone before I start taking this?" I asked, holding up the crumpled square of paper in my hand.

He looked up at me, eyebrows raised. "Of course," he said, scooting his chair on their casters to the bookshelf on the wall next to him. "If interested, you might also take a look at this." He handed me a book from his meager collection that would change my life forever: *Feeling Good: The New Mood Therapy* by David D. Burns (Burns, 1980). I didn't fill the prescription he gave me and never took an antidepressant or other mood-enhancing drug. Burns' book helped me understand how my thoughts, perceptions, and beliefs are responsible for my moods. I learned the feelings I have at any moment are due to my thoughts I've just been thinking. It taught me how to step back from my thoughts, consider them for what they are—just thoughts—and challenge where they came from.

The good doctor did set me up with a therapist, and a few weeks later I sat through my first—and last—session of talk therapy. I was cautious and wary walking down the long, narrow hall to her office that day. Reminiscent of those movie scenes where the path in front of the character keeps getting longer and longer, it seemed I would never reach the end and would have to start running to make any progress. Except I didn't run. I just looked around dubiously. It reminded me of a moment from my childhood feeling I was the only one on earth; everyone else was a robot, and I was just a specimen to observe. Maybe this was a kind of "flash forward" because the visit remains a bit surreal to me, in hindsight.

I sat in the dark but comfortable room across the desk from the smiling, youngish therapist. I'll call her Gina. In my memory of the visit, something obscures Gina's face. Maybe a desk lamp? I'm not sure, but the memory must be some symbol of my hesitancy to open up and bare my soul to this perfectly amiable stranger. We talked about my feelings, me describing my life at the moment, what I did in a typical day. We obviously hadn't established any rapport in that short time, but it seemed Gina had figured out how to help me in no less than forty-five minutes. She confidently instructed me at the end of the visit to, "Go make some friends and come back in two weeks to see me."

I didn't make friends. I didn't know *how* to make friends. I didn't *have* friends (which is, I'm pretty sure why she told me to "go make some"). I worked part time from home for an agency 150 miles away, and when not "busy" clocking in there and taking care of the needs of a baby, I was immovable in my bed. I knew when I left Gina's office making friends wasn't going to happen, and certainly not in two weeks. I cancelled my next appointment and never returned.

I imagine a somewhat similar scenario of my mom and feelings she may have had during her life raising us girls. She didn't have a college education. I don't believe she ever saw a therapist or doctor for any mental health issue. In some part of my mind, I mimicked her life, doing what I saw played out by her in front of me as a child. My mom spent hours in her bedroom many afternoons "taking a nap," as she'd say, quite believable with five children so close in age. But the numbness she emitted, the laughter and joy I rarely saw her express, leads me to wonder about her unhappiness and possible depression. Thinking about her life this way and having personal experience with depression helps me have empathy for my mom and how she raised us.

The book the psychiatrist steered me toward that day in his office helped me understand where my depression came from. It gave me ways to think differently about depression and separate it from my entirety. What I learned didn't "cure" me—if such a word can be used in a mental health context—but loosened the hold it had on me and helped me accept part of myself. This first of many books and articles I devoured began my journey through self-discovery and growth that continues today.

I never again sank to the depths I did in those early years, struggling to get out of bed or take action, although my black dog continued to follow me and does to this day. He's a Rottweiler named Fido; we've become friends.

NUMBNESS

———

"The problem isn't how hard you're working, it's that you're working on things that aren't right for you. Your goals and motivations aren't harmonizing with your deepest truth. They didn't come from your own inclinations. They came from the two forces that drive us all off our true paths: trauma and socialization."

—MARTHA BECK, *THE WAY OF INTEGRITY*

I continuously mulled over my sister Colleen's remark to me: "Why is someone with a master's degree in engineering working at the Sheriff's Office?" After a brief eighteen-month stint at the DNR, I abandoned any semblance of the engineering workforce or other employment while awaiting the birth of our second daughter, Madison. Household finances tight, I floundered a bit with freelancing transcription services and took a job as a 9-1-1 call taker, alternating night shifts for a couple years. I focused on being the best mother I could, while contributing to keeping our household finances afloat. But the internal nagging continued, echoing the failure to fulfill my potential and the external shaming—Colleen's comment stung. I had a graduate degree, after all, but seemed to have thrown all those years, all the effort and dollars, away to do … what? I still didn't know.

In hindsight, I don't believe Colleen meant to be mean. She, after all, had grown up in the same household as I with emotionally distant parents and experienced the death of a sibling. If these things affected her in any way at all like they did me, I must give grace to her and all my sisters for how we behave and the things we say as adults.

When our son, Will, came along, I intentionally put plans for my personal path and purpose on hold to raise our three beautiful children. I threw myself into their activities and development. By the time our kids were in elementary school, we had moved to a larger house, and Bryce worked hard to allow me to stay home with them. I have no regrets about putting my children first for so many years, seeing it as a privilege and sacred responsibility. But I had put my needs as a human being on a back burner and shoved down my own feelings, emotions and needs in a dark, bottomless bag. This could not and would not be suppressed but expressed outwardly to the detriment of my family—and to my embarrassment in confessing it—in many ways.

When my kids were very young, I would join them during their daily nap or quiet time. Later, when they were older and didn't need constant watching, I'd just take naps. Scarred by my own mother's door-slamming exasperation and huff into her bedroom to sleep in the middle of the day, I simply told my kids I would be in my bedroom if they needed anything. I didn't need an excuse for my naps. Taking care of three children was hard work. Surely anyone would agree a nap now and then was to be expected and excused. But my naps were more than a catch up of missed slumber. My naps were a blot out, an escape, a way to not have to think beyond the immediate numbness inside me.

That numbness, the inability to understand or express how I felt, manifested in anger at myself for not being more than I was. The expectation of "doing something with my life" just because I graduated college and grad school burdened me. It also surfaced through occasional outbursts with my family.

My kids were around preteen age when I looked for the scissors one day in our kitchen. The small drawer below the counter and next to the wall telephone housed extra keys, Scotch tape, pencils and pens, and a pair of silver household scissors. I don't know why I needed them. I don't know the "urgency" of which I had to have them, but they weren't in the drawer where they were supposed to live, and I flipped out. Feeling the anger boiling in my stomach and up into my chest, I stomped around the kitchen wall into the hallway and asked in a huff, "Where are the scissors?"

Curled up and sitting across the room on the sofa, Haley shifted her eyes from her book to look up at me. She somberly shook her head. Maddie and Will just looked at me in silence, eyes wide, from playing games. I said a little bit louder, "Where are the scissors? They are supposed to be right here in the drawer!" I turned back around to the kitchen and rummaged the drawer once again. Not finding them, I yelled through the kitchen wall, "Why is nothing ever where it is supposed to be in this house?" I slammed the drawer shut and threw some silverware in the sink. Leaning upright into the counter, I took a deep breath and tried to calm down. From the other room I heard the kids quietly skedaddle to their rooms. "Argh!" I snarled, storming to my bedroom and slamming the door shut behind me.

When broaching the subject of my naps and occasional outbursts with my children now, they shrug it off, either pretending not to remember or not seeing it as significant in their lives, at least for them in their twenties. Maybe I'm just feeding into the insecurity about my parental imperfections, waking up the old Catholic guilt residing in my psyche at all times as an unwelcome recluse. Maddie remembers me "going to my bedroom" and thinking or knowing as a kid not to disturb me; this was my quiet time. "Whenever you were in your bedroom, you were dealing with something," she told me later.

Bryce recalls an afternoon when thirteen-year-old Haley called him at work crying. "Dad, can you come home?" she begged.

"Yes, baby. What's wrong?" he said.

"Can you just come home?" she pleaded. When Bryce walked into the house, he first saw Will sitting at the high kitchen counter playing his Gameboy and eating crackers with the TV on low in the living room.

"What's up, buddy?" Bryce said, looking around the house cautiously. The house screamed with inaudible tension.

"Hi Dad!" Will chirped, sounding a little too chipper.

"What's going on?" Bryce asked, noticing the closed bedroom doors.

"I dunno," shrugged Will, focusing his attention back to his game. Bryce walked over and knocked on Maddie's bedroom door. When he peeked in, Haley sat in one corner of the room and Maddie in the other, both on the floor, backs to the wall knees up to their chins. They were still crying.

"Is anybody hurt? Bleeding?" he asked as he walked over and sat on the bed facing them.

"It's Mom," they both sobbed. Some exchange had occurred between us that day, but no one can remember what.

Bryce calmed them down and then came into our bedroom and sat with me.

Although events like this were not common, a haze of tension hanging over the household was. I take full responsibility. I kept house as my mother did.

My goal for my children has always been for them to be independent, responsible adults, and I am proud of who they have become—intelligent, self-assured and delightful. But I am not the perfect mother or ideal role model, as my mother before me wasn't to me and my sisters growing up.

When my children were older and full time in school, I applied for part-time work at a local nonprofit, my graduate degree coming in handy. I learned the executive director thought it a valued achievement, even though the organization worked in healthcare. I didn't get the connection, but I did get the job and have worked in the sector ever since, although now for an education-related organization. I also kept busy shuttling my kids to after-school and evening soccer, volleyball, T-ball, lacrosse, band and choral concerts, church youth group meetings, and a myriad of other activities. I saw how my sisters and I were susceptible to getting into trouble with nothing to do after school, and I made sure that didn't happen to my kids. Although I resisted the label "soccer mom," I unwittingly became just that.

Never the PTA mom or classroom volunteer of the year, my job (thankfully) kept me from those types of commitments, I did for some reason—some temporary bout of insanity—become manager of Haley's youth soccer team and then Will's. I kept just as busy as my kids.

Back then I'd leave work at three o'clock and head over to Will's middle school to take my turn in the car pick up line. Will would saunter out by himself, squinting in the sun, his too-big backpack weighing his skinny body into an arc. I'd get out and open the car's liftgate. "How was your day, bud?" I'd say as he'd sling his pack into the car.

"Fine," Will would shrug with indifference. My arm above my head and resting on the hatch, I'd look around the school yard trying to spot any of the other boys we had to take to the soccer field. I'd smile as they'd find us, one by one, throwing their gear on top of each other's.

"Hi, Mrs. Burger," they'd each say with preadolescent awkwardness, heads down, trying not to make eye contact. I'd smile and chuckle as they bantered with each other about their day, smack-talking and giggling in the back seat.

One boy would inevitably unzip his gym bag and pull out his cleats. "Ugh! Put that thing away. You're gonna stink us out!" the others would moan as the odor quickly permeated the inside of the vehicle. Although easily ninety degrees outside, I'd open the car windows so we could breathe. I loved these times in the car, grateful for the glimpse into my kids' daily lives.

When we landed at the soccer field, the boys would bail out of the car and grab their bags, walking up the slope to their coach and teammates. In the two hours before practice ended, I'd either rush to pick up Maddie or Haley at one of their activities or make a quick trip to the nearest Publix Super Market or Walgreens store. Sometimes I would be able to find a shady spot in the parking lot away from the other parents and cars and take a catnap. When the kids were older and Haley was driving, I would go for a run around the park during practice. On the sideline of Haley's soccer games, I connected with a couple other moms with whom I've made lifelong friends (therapist Gina would be proud!).

This time in my life—engaging in my children's activities and lives, reaching out and making true friendships—marked the beginning of a turnaround in me, making sure my needs were met, my soul taken care of. The afternoon naps largely disappeared or were an actual luxury on the rare lazy weekend afternoons and not a means of escape from any numbness. During this time, I started exercising again more regularly, running and biking, taking on home video aerobics and yoga. Some sort of cloud began to lift, and I felt I could see for the first time in a while. Then the storm hit.

MONSOON SEASON BEGINS

"Yes, these are times of great illness and distress. Yet the center may just hold."

—ANNE LAMOTT, *DUSK, NIGHT, DAWN*

Family screws up any individuality or separateness I some-times long for, the desire to have no responsibilities to another person in this world, the just-leave-me-alone-and-take-care-of-yourself feeling I want to have. Children, parents, siblings can do this to us. Letting go, severing the bond, and cutting the last infinitesimally tiny umbilical cord thread tying us together is impossible. When something happens to them, it happens to us as well. Ready or not, here it comes. As I've learned from Joseph Campbell, "There is no separateness" (Campbell, 2008). He is right. I can either resist it with every atom in my body and remain small, or embrace it, open myself up, and grow into my humanness.

In 2008, just as I began leaning into my life, finally glimpsing how I might fit into this world, those family ties called my bluff. If the Morton Salt slogan "When it rains, it pours" is true, then a six-year long monsoon rainy season where I felt, more than ever, the tie to family and children had begun. It all started with my son.

Will, a happy, congenial child, playful and well-liked, enjoyed a typical relationship with his older sisters. He pestered them when he wanted attention and allowed them to wrestle him down in annoyed laughter when he took it too far. His friends called him "iTunes" because he knew every popular song, either singing, humming, or whistling one whenever they hung out with him for more than a few minutes. Sitting at the kitchen table playing games as a family, we didn't need any music playing from an external source. We had Will. He didn't seem to realize his vocalization of these internal recitals. During one round of Uno, I recorded him sitting there, looking at his cards, and crooning away. We still have a good laugh thinking about those times.

On our way back home from seeing *Pirates of the Caribbean* at a local theater one early summer afternoon, we chatted about our favorite scenes from the movie. Ten-year-old Will sat directly behind me in the back seat muttering to himself. Not hearing or understanding him, I turned around to face him.

"That was a line from the movie. I didn't say that. I just copied from the movie," he muttered, over and over again.

"What are you doing, Will?" I asked, trying to understand what he had just said and why.

"Uh, nothing. Nothing," he said, shifting his pained expression to the window and tapping his fingers on his knees. I turned with a concerned look at Bryce in the driver's seat. He just shrugged, keeping his eyes on the road. Haley and Maddie didn't seem to notice the mumbling.

Later that summer, Will stayed with his grandparents for a couple weeks. My husband's parents treated each of their grandchildren to a trip to Chicago, followed by a week in Iowa, when the kids turned ten. Gazing out the second-story window of his grandparents' home one day, Will watched the ruby-throated hummingbirds dart in and out of the bright red feeder mounted to the exterior wooden deck in plain view. Leaning his belly into the back of a chair and looking past the seat's headrest, he sorrowfully dropped his head on his arm and shared solemnly through tears to his grandmother, "I've lost my joy."

As a mother, hearing this about my preadolescent child—especially my youngest—crushed my heart and strained the umbilical cord tether between us. I wanted to protect him from life, cover him up so the big harsh world couldn't get to him. I wanted him to stay young and innocent forever.

I shrugged this off as Will just starting adolescence and experiencing an unfamiliar melancholy preteen mood. I wish that's all it had been. In hindsight, I recognize Will's singing and humming had lessened and his muttering to himself had increased. Not thinking much about it at the time, I didn't know what I could or should do, so I shrugged it off.

Later in the fall, Will sat at the kitchen table working on his homework. He concentrated on the same page for thirty minutes, writing and erasing, writing and erasing. I saw him struggling—frowning, eyebrows furled—and heard his sighs. Cutting some vegetables for dinner, I looked up and saw the hole he had rubbed in the newsprint. He started to cry.

"What's wrong?" I came over to him, trying to see how I could help.

"I don't want to plagiarize," he sobbed.

Later I learned the previous spring a policeman had come to his school classroom and talked to students about cheating and mentioned plagiarism. That day at the table, Will believed he was plagiarizing and would go to jail. That summer in the car repeating lines from the movie, he believed he was plagiarizing the actors' lines. Seemingly silly to me, Will's mind had made a "rule" of not cheating and had irrationally thrown up the "red alert" signal at any sign of violating the rule. The image of Will's face at the table that day—distorted and lined in anguish like a tortured old man in a Salvador Dalí painting—told me something was seriously wrong. I needed to figure out what.

The next day I made an appointment for Will with a school psychologist we knew and began to do some researching. I suspected he suffered from obsessive-compulsive disorder, and our appointment confirmed it.

A couple of weeks after the homework incident, Bryce, Will, and I sat on the flower-print sofa in the living room of the psychologist's home office. She kindly, and with a motherly tone, asked Will questions. "Do you feel sad, mad, hopeless, stuck, or something else?" and "How often do you feel this way? What helps to make these feelings go away?"

After he answered the best he could, and Bryce and I chirped in from our points of view, she said calmly, "I think you have some anxiety, which just means you worry a lot about things. Here are some exercises you can do—ways to think about your worries," she said, handing Will a blue folder with some papers inside. "Your mom can help." Reaching into the pocket of her oversized dress, she pulled out a small, smooth, gray rock.

"Here. Take this," she said, taking his small hand and placing the rock in his palm, closing his fingers around it.

"Put this in your pocket, and whenever you feel upset, put your hand in your pocket, and rub your fingers on the rock. This is your worry stone."

"Okay," Will said, glancing at me, eyebrows raised.

"Come here, Will, and stand right in front of me," she directed Will calmly. He complied, and she began gently tapping his forehead and temples. Will's eyes shifted to me, his head and face unmoved. I detected some alarm in his expression.

"Whenever you feel worried, you can gently tap your face like this. This helps to reset your brain and calm down," she finished, sitting back in her lounge chair. "I believe Will has an anxiety disorder called obsessive-compulsive disorder. These materials and the tapping should help, but come back in a couple weeks to check in."

We left her "office" and got in the car. I turned in my seat to look back at Will buckling his seat belt. He looked up at me and said, "That was weird, Mom."

"I know," I responded, turning to put the car in gear.

Unsettled by this particular psychologist's self-soothing suggestions, I embarked on further research—similar to the one I did into depression—to learn everything I could about OCD in children and how to manage. This took me on a circuitous and frustrating route, including a shrug from Will's pediatrician and an offer for a Zoloft prescription, lengthy internet searches, and the purchase and reading of several books about the disorder. I learned although OCD can occur at any age, it generally tends to first appear between the ages of eight and twelve, or between the late teen years and early adulthood. About one in two hundred kids and teens have OCD, about the same number who have diabetes (International OCD Foundation, 2022).

Through the International OCD Foundation, I eventually discovered a resource the pediatrician didn't know about right in our backyard—the University of Florida Child Psychology Department's OCD Program. The psychologist we met here—Dr. Joe, as we call him—became a godsend to us, and finding him was life changing for Will. Will began a journey of exposure and response prevention therapy (ERP or CBT-E/RP) which continues fourteen years later.

The essence of ERP is to expose a person to the fear causing the obsession—a little at a time and in a safe space. This allows the brain to calm to the perceived threat and be able to move past it without completing a compulsive behavior. Will's earliest obsessions were thinking he was plagiarizing everything he said or wrote—resulting in the excessive muttering and excuses about a phrase he had just uttered and the holes in his homework page, and believing he contaminated the ground with every step he took, killing all the grass and insects beneath him. This became a significant problem for a child who loved competing in his young team's soccer tournaments.

At the end of the first week of Will's intense, week-long therapy visit, Dr. Joe and I followed about fifteen feet behind him while walking to our car parked a block away in the campus garage. Sobbing uncontrollably, Will looked back at us every few steps. His expression seemed to say, "How can you make me do this? Make this stop," but also held the tiniest bit of trust and hope the smarter adults in his life wouldn't completely abandon him and knew what they were making him do.

The five-minute walk took twenty. "I can't do this," Will agonized.

We stopped every time he turned around. He had to face his fear of unwittingly stepping on an ant or other insect, thinking if he did, he would be molesting it in some way. Dr. Joe assured me Will had no idea at his age what that meant, only it was harmful to another being. Will also knew what else Dr. Joe was asking him to do once we got back to the car.

Opening the rear hatch of our Highlander revealed an apprehensive lizard nestled in the shavings of his oversized crate, a lighting and heating apparatus, plastic container of live mealyworms, and an old blanket. Will's fifth grade teacher kept reptile terrariums in her classroom and let students take care of them at home over long school breaks. It was the beginning of the two-week winter holiday break and Will's turn to take care of Spike, the bearded dragon. Although excited by the privilege, when it came time to actually bring the lizard home, he became panic stricken.

I turned to look at Will. We waited while he, still racking, cautiously reached up to touch the top of Spike's cage. He did so, knowing he had to hold his hand there long enough for the anxiety to subside. Dr. Joe stood, hands in his black pants pocket. I stood in my jacket, purse slung over my shoulder, waiting patiently in the echoing parking garage. It took several minutes, but Will's breathing began to subside, and the tears stopped.

We said goodbye to Dr. Joe, also heading into a school break, knowing we wouldn't see him over the holiday. Will and I got in the car.

"How do you feel about all that?" I asked him.

"I can't talk about it anymore. I'm just tired." His body sagged in his seat, head against the door window. We were heading into a long two weeks.

This type of therapy relieved a tremendous amount of Will's suffering, but took substantial time, effort and emotion to get through. It continued for several years. Will still uses some tools today; some periods are more intense and draining than others. As with depression, OCD is something people live with and are never really "cured" of.

Reflecting on this time with Will, I recognize parallels with how my parents responded to my sister Jenny's cerebral palsy and eventual cancer diagnosis. They dove in, dedicating endless time and energy to support her needs. They felt the familial tie and responded to it, unable to resist its pull. I can appreciate that now and better understand how they were tied to my sisters and me, how they did love us. Somehow, we couldn't understand that their actions revealed their love more than words. As children, though, we needed to hear the love, not just observe it.

That same fall, up in Iowa, my dad's health faded. He had survived ten years post-surgical removal of a cancerous lung tumor and subsequent radiation therapy for a metastasized brain tumor, but his body was giving out. His balance failing, Mom found herself calling 9-1-1 multiple times when she couldn't get him up off the bathroom floor after a tumble.

Mom had her share of health challenges that same year, too. She had suffered with rheumatoid arthritis for a couple of decades and now osteoporosis was taking its toll on her bones, causing hip fractures and resultant hospital stays and wildly protested wheelchair restrictions. She also had a recent hysterectomy after a routine pelvic exam revealed cancerous cells in her ovaries.

Neither of them well, they resisted the home health care services we tried to arrange for them. We girls were living and working in five different parts of the country—Kelly the closest, two-hours away by car in Des Moines—unable to drop our lives to assist in any long-term manner. Inevitably, Dad moved to an assisted living facility—thankfully just a mile from East Shaulis Road—for personal care in getting bathed and dressed and other around the clock assistance with daily living.

So, along with managing the early days of Will's OCD therapy, the tether to my parents woke up, growing increasingly taut as their health waned. I flew up to Iowa a handful of times to support Mom and Dad as best I could, taking Dad to doctors' visits and putting up with Mom's complaints about the state of her decrepit body. Assisting Dad with his walker on one such visit, I helped him navigate the uneven sidewalk and double doors of the medical building entrance. Dad smiled and waved to the young receptionist and other office staff as if they were lifelong, childhood friends. Everyone responded to his conviviality in kind and took good care of him in his faltering state.

I can't recall the specific reason for the visit—just one of many such appointments on his calendar—but I remember walking to the check-out counter and Dad saying he had to use the restroom. The kind nurse walked him slowly to the nearby room as I waited outside. We soon heard a "thunk," and when the staff opened the door, we saw Dad on the floor with a surprised look on his face, pants down around his ankles, trying to get up. Seeing his vulnerable and humiliating position solidified in my mind the finality of his current state, and I shared his helplessness in the moment, my chest burned. With the help of the office staff, Dad recovered, joking in disbelief of what just happened to him, brushing it off as a "just another day" event.

The last time I saw Dad alive he sat at the dining room of the assisted living facility with a few friends. In his old age he still didn't know a stranger and, in my mind, craved such interaction after years living alone with Mom. I came over to say goodbye before I left for the airport to fly home. I chatted with his table guests, and they sadly remarked to Dad, "It's so nice that your daughters come to visit you here. Mine never do."

I kissed Dad on his bald, shiny head, and he said, "Love you, Boo. Thanks for coming."

He died that spring less than a month later in hospice, alone in his bed wearing his Green Bay Packers sweatshirt.

For some reason, Mom called and told Bryce that Dad had died. Apparently, she couldn't or didn't want to tell me directly, a fact that still perturbs me today. When I learned Dad was gone, I curled up on top of my bed and cried. In the movie, *Divine Secrets of the Ya-Ya Sisterhood*, Sidda asks her dad—after being reunited and before meeting with her mother—"Daddy, did you get loved enough?" (Khouri, 2002) It's a question I always wonder about my own father.

For more than a decade, Mom and Dad traveled to Florida for a couple months each winter to escape the Iowa weather. Never considering land-locked Gainesville, they rented a house or condo on a beach along one of the coasts less than a two-hour drive away. Too infrequently we visited them on weekends, but the kids enjoyed fishing off their dock in Cedar Key, playing on the sand on Vilano Beach or just goofing off with their grandpa and laughing at the Hernando Beach pelicans diving from the air into the water like torpedoes toward their unsuspecting lunch.

Thinking about Mom moving to Florida after Dad passed wasn't a stretch. She had confided to Jill a few years earlier she wanted to move to Florida, but Dad wasn't ready—not ready either because his mother remained alive and nearby or because his health was on an uncertain downhill since his cancer diagnosis.

The year before Dad passed, when he was too ill to come to Florida one winter, Mom came down to spend some time with our kids and get a break from the cold and full-time care of her husband. Looking for her to walk through the Orlando International Airport arrival gate, I was shocked to see—and didn't recognize—the frail, gray-haired lady limping toward us. *When did Mom get to be so old and slight?* I remember thinking. My mind's picture of my mother had always been strong and impenetrable, and this was someone else entirely. Instant compassion for her overcame me, something I didn't recognize with her before. The "red alert" tug of our common tie nagged at me.

Because of Mom's uncertain health, her staying at East Shaulis Road by herself after Dad passed became an impossible option. I don't remember the exact conversation, but my sisters and I agreed—kind of knew—Mom should move to Florida near Bryce and me. She resisted the initial suggestion of leaving her home of forty-plus years, but no big argument ensued. She valued her independence, but I imagine behind her tough exterior facade she was terrified of living alone. But whether the idea of finally living in Florida or the exhaustion of years of caring for, then burying, her husband of fifty-three years tipped the scales. She acquiesced, and we sisters came together to help pack up the house.

Several weeks later, we had sorted through a lifetime, giving away, trashing, or yard-selling everything inside the huge home. In my mind we all turned on the "doing" part of our brain—as we learned from our mother—and blocked out our feelings. We took care of the job at hand—sorting and organizing Mom's old life to fit her new one. I don't remember big moments of grief or nostalgia coming over us. We did the work in front of us. Not that we didn't care about our father just dying. It was there right under the surface. I could feel it. We just didn't know how to express it.

Standing in the driveway looking at the dozen or so folding tables, boxes, and tarps stacked with memories of our family's life, Colleen walked over to a Packer's blanket she had given Dad and lifted it up for one last look. She put it down, turning her head to the ground, eyes closed. Colleen's gesture echoed how painful this was, regardless of how efficient and diligent we were being in sorting, cleaning, and organizing.

Silent, Mom walked back into the house, doubtless going in for another cigarette. Mom was stoic about Dad's passing—I never saw her break down about her loss. Like her, none of us knew how to express our emotions. We had learned it from her.

I've since read big, life-altering decisions should not be made for at least six months following the death of a loved one or other traumatic event in one's life. I imagine every end-of-life "expert" shaking their head at how we managed to upend Mom's life just a few weeks after Dad died. We just didn't see any other option at the time. Just as I had a turbulent year, Mom had too. I'm not sure she ever really recovered.

MOM IN GAINESVILLE

"Many of us have not had even adequate mothering, much less the ideal; many of our mothers have been too depleted themselves. We end up disappointed in our mothers, hurt, angry, blaming, needy, raging, yet unable to let go of our need for them. We feel starved emotionally and try to cover that over. We feel terrified of becoming like our mothers and vow to be different with our children. We end up estranged from our mothers and estranged from ourselves. We carry around an unhealed child; a sense of woundedness and of longing that seems to have nowhere to go."

—KATHIE CARLSON, *IN HER IMAGE*

Mom moved to Gainesville the summer of 2009 and stayed with Bryce and me for a couple weeks as we shopped for a permanent home for her. She pushed for a small home by herself, but her finances dictated otherwise. The monthly John Deere pension and Social Security payments were sufficient for monthly survival and comfort, but her savings were limited. The thought of helping her manage the upkeep of a homestead made Bryce and my hearts skip a beat and blood pressures rise. We could hardly keep up with our own. I thought she also needed company, other people, a community, socialization, and again, in my mind, to be happy.

The Village, the senior living community we moved Mom to, touted the tag line, "Retirement, the way it should be." It offered every amenity you could think of plus several options for independent living, from efficiencies and one- and two-bedroom apartments, to two-bedroom freestanding cottages. Mom remained silent as we sped along the community's smooth, quiet streets and sidewalks that warm June day. The friendly sales representative, experienced at navigating the network of paths and lanes in the golf cart, took us to the two residential apartments we had chosen based on Mom's finances. Smelling of paint and drywall, we walked onto the plastic runner protecting the carpet of the one-bedroom unit in the newly built The Cypress. As we toured the one-bedroom unit looking out over a small lake and woods from the third-floor balcony, Mom snipped, "It's too small." We jumped back in the cart to tour the Tower Club across the street, home to all dining, wellness, and activity services, where a few residents were roving about. Mom, shoulders back and head up, used her cane to slowly keep up with us on the burgundy patterned, industrial carpet. She said nothing as we looked from the hallway through the glass wall to the large pool and decking, cafeteria behind us.

Mom often smiled as she spoke about her days before marriage to Dad. She had also declared to Jill a few years earlier he held them back from moving to Florida. So, we were sure Mom would eagerly embrace a life of new friends, new "adventures." But she didn't. She was a big talker on that front. She was a turtle sticking her head out of its shell to see her surroundings, taking a slow cautious step, just to scurry back into her shell when something moved too quickly around her. That shell acted as her safe haven and was impenetrable to anyone. Michael Singer in *The Untethered Soul* (Singer, 2007) describes some people as having painful, psychological thorns protruding from them. If someone comes too close, the person will do everything they can to protect themselves from the closeness, the pain. Mom seemed like that. No one could get too close to her, or she would retreat to her hardened shell of anger and vitriol aimed at no one but everyone at the same time.

I'm not sure how she became this person. I've acknowledged she was never the lovey-dovey, hugs and kisses, here-let-me-comfort-you-sweetie kind of mother, but growing up I don't recall the everyday vehemence of her anger or this level of unhappiness. True, she had just lost her husband, been reluctantly upended from her home of over forty years, and spent the last twenty plus years in chronic pain. I guess in a similar situation I would be a bit cranky, too. In hindsight I get it. I understand. I can empathize. Later on into her tenure in Gainesville, the companion we hired to sit with her a couple days a week shamed me. With her calm, angelic demeanor, she seemed to have so much patience, so much compassion for Mom, becoming—albeit for a short time—friends and, I suspect, Mom's confidant. But for a daughter, dragging her own baggage and unresolved neglected emotional history on her shoulders, trying to support, love, and care for such a person daily, was an impossible task—at least for me.

But I thought it would be different. I had this idyllic image in my head I would rise to the occasion, brush off Mom's verbal abuse, and not be deeply offended and hurt by it all. She uttered a gruff, "Where have you been?" then glared and turned her back to me when I entered her apartment; this stabbed me in the heart. Her incessant, "I need …," "Go get me …," and "Why didn't you …" demands wore me down. I thought that I had matured enough to take her on. I thought I could provide some sort of geriatric paradise for her—one with friends her age, a bus to drive her to activities both nearby and a day's trip away, and a life that my sisters and I thought she wanted and would thrive in. I thought I was brilliant for finding her a well-kempt independent living community she could afford with "resort-quality amenities including a heated outdoor pool, spa, tennis courts, a health and fitness center, three restaurants offering fine dining, café-style dining, and a full-service lounge." I thought all this wonder could absolve me of the guilt of not paying more attention to her and Dad over the past several years, the too-few phone calls checking-in on them, the resistance I had to taking care of their emotional needs when I couldn't even identify my own.

But I was incredulous what was offered to her never seemed right, never seemed to satisfy the hole inside needing filling. She found something wrong with everything. When she first moved to Gainesville, I helped her get groceries at Publix to stock her refrigerator. In the middle of the day, the store was fairly quiet. Mom leaned over the cart handle for balance, looking left and right at the well-stocked shelves as we walked in silence down each aisle. "I need to get some berries," she said as we turned toward the produce section.

She was resistant to any help from me with loading items into her cart. She was particular about her produce, examining each piece and package before putting in her cart, and barked at me if my choices weren't suitable. I walked to the end of the series of bins and grabbed a small bunch of bananas, remembering that earlier she said she needed them.

As I put them at the bottom of her cart, she chided, "Oh, Tracy! Those are green!" She grabbed them and ambled down the aisle, holding the bananas out in one arm for balance. She put them back and picked up an equally green bunch from the options and threw them in the cart. I ended up just walking a step behind her the rest of the visit. She knew what she wanted and didn't appear to need my interference in any way.

After a grueling twenty minutes we finally made it to the checkout area where only two lanes were open, and two shoppers were waiting in each. "Ugh," she said tersely, rolling her eyes and parking behind a middle-aged man and his cart. "Why don't they open another lane? This town is so backward." The man in front of us turned his head to look at us, eyebrows lifted.

Except for her huffing, we inched our way silently to the young, slight cashier who said, "Hi, there. Sorry for your wait. Did you find everything you needed?"

"I need some Kool menthols. A carton," Mom said gruffly, waving her hand in the direction of customer service where the cigarettes were stowed and digging around in her purse for her wallet. I smiled apologetically. The cashier looked down, scanning Mom's items a little faster. Walking to her car, I was instantly transported back to being a teenager, following behind her, the child once again. I could feel myself close to her, a numbness overcoming me. I couldn't say or do anything to reach her, and the thought of trying any more exhausted me.

We settled Mom in a one-bedroom, nine-hundred-square-foot apartment on the bottom floor of a beautiful, plantation-style, three-floor apartment in Magnolia Grand. It had a screened-in porch, fully equipped kitchen, living room, and washer and dryer. We flew Mom down to stay with us after Dad died, so Colleen, Rhonda, and Rhonda's boyfriend packed and drove her car down in a caravan with a small U-Haul truck loaded with the lifetime of belongings we all guessed she would need and want in her new and much-downsized world.

As the last of the boxes were brought in, the apartment humid and hot from the door being open, I stood next to Mom and looked over her new living space, familiar furniture placed exactly where she wanted. She ambled through the living room and looked out the sliding glass doors to the empty porch. She didn't have a porch on East Shaulis Road.

"We'll have to get some furniture out there for you," I said hopefully.

She nodded quietly, turned her head down, and walked past me to sit at a dining table chair. Her body sagged in the chair, and she looked defeated. "Why can't I just go back home?" she asked, looking up at me with puppy dog eyes.

"You can't, Mom. You know that," I'd remind her more than once the first year she lived here.

I checked on her frequently those first few weeks, going to lunch with her in the cafeteria and taking short walks around Ibis Landing on the 104-acre wooded property. I encouraged her to sign up for one of the outings offered to residents weekly, and she joined a handful during her five-year tenure there. I looked forward to hearing of her day trip to Cedar Key, a fishing town about an hour and a half drive west from Gainesville, for lunch and shopping. She and Dad had snowbirded there two consecutive years, vacationing there a few months during the Iowa winters, and I thought she would enjoy visiting the familiar, quaint coastal town.

"How was the trip, Mom?" I asked the next day.

"We had to wait for everyone to load and unload the bus. One guy, Charlie, was late boarding and we sat on the bus for twenty minutes waiting for him. We should have just left him there," she bitched. She didn't seem to enjoy the trip and let a seemingly minor inconvenience ruin it for her.

I heard almost weekly about the overcooked vegetables served at the cafeteria. I choked back a laugh when she declared in an indignant voice, "There are too many old people who live here." She was only seventy-three and most of the other residents were well into their eighties. She complained cleaning staff were intrusive and didn't even speak English. She found the university town's worship of everything "Gator" stupid.

Once when Colleen came down for a visit, Mom ordered shrimp scampi at a local restaurant. "Look! The tails are still on them. How are we supposed to eat these?" she snipped indignantly. She looked up for the waiter.

"Excuse me," she called across the room, gaining the harried waiter's attention.

"These shrimps still have the tails on them. How am I supposed to eat them?" she barked.

The waiter took a step back in surprise, looking at the rest of us. "That's just the way they come, ma'am," he said slowly.

"You've got to be kidding me," she laughed, shaking her head. "Oh, never mind!"

We tried to explain to her it was customary to leave the tails on and she could cut them with her knife, but she would not agree. I was mortified and especially embarrassed because my in-laws had joined us for lunch. She embarrassed me more than once in public. Nothing was right, and nobody could do anything to make it right.

One day, a couple weeks after she had moved in, I came for a visit. Mom sat in the driver's seat of her red Buick

LeSabre smoking a cigarette, door open, one foot on the parking lot asphalt. Dad cherished and took great care of his cars, upgrading every three to four years as suggested by the local Waterloo dealership. I imagine Mom saw the car as a symbol of independence and a comforting memory of life with Dad; they put a lot of miles on their vehicles over the years together driving down to Florida each winter. The Village prohibited smoking in any of the apartment units, and Mom had taken to claiming the parking spot closest to her unit and "sneaking" a smoke (or twenty) every day.

During a visit the next week I found her puffing away inside her apartment smiling with an arrogant smirk on her face. "Bob said I should have the right to smoke in my apartment and not have to hide out in my car," she quipped with a pucker of lips and exhale of nicotine exhaust. Bob was a neighbor down the walkway. After that, I hit a cloud of dense smoke when entering the small apartment and required a shower upon returning home. I recall an EMT's concern upon approaching her unit once when called to assist her after a fall, "Where's the fire?" And years after Mom passed away, a friend of ours, the facilities manager at The Village, could identify Mom's apartment by the still lingering odor of stale third-hand cigarette smoke.

I nagged Mom about her smoking, teaming up with her doctors in emphasizing how detrimental smoking was to bone health and possible contributions to her rheumatoid arthritis (RA) symptoms. I pushed her to make friends and wanted Mom to finally be happy, content. I wanted her to take care of herself. I wanted all her vices to miraculously disappear. I wanted her to find her life worth living. Maybe I wanted all these things for her just to know they were possible for me. Supposedly my role model for living, I couldn't accept a life of pain, both physical and emotional might be in the cards for either her or me. I resisted understanding my inability to change her, my lack of control over how she lived her life. I kept resisting and pressing on as if I could make everything better for her. By making things better for her, maybe my life wasn't doomed to unhappiness and depression. I needed that to be true. Somehow, I needed her to find happiness so I could find my own. I could then move on to care for myself. But this was the ultimate lie.

While Mom griped to me about everything when we were together, she transformed into a different person around other people. She lit up like a spark when her grandchildren came for visits. She'd lay out the red carpet of snacks—snacks they certainly didn't get at my house. All three of my kids remember going to her place after soccer practice during the week or on Sunday afternoons, sitting around the coffee table chowing down on Fritos chips and cheese dip and the endless supply of chocolate candies she'd haul out. They helped her navigate Facebook and troubleshoot any computer problems she might be experiencing. Mom proudly showed her grandkids off to the other residents at the lunch cafeteria where everyone would fawn over them. For special occasions, we'd make reservations for Sunday brunch in the dining room. Mom, donned in her "best" dress, lifted her head as she sauntered to our table looking around for any acquaintances she could introduce to her grandchildren.

Mom did make a few fast friends at The Village—Margie, a sassy woman who could keep up with Mom's wine habit, and Shirley, a proud southern woman who flinched at every perceived ache and pain. They met her for lunch and dinner and introduced her to some folks at the lounge over cocktails.

We brought two of Mom's coveted sewing machines down from Iowa—a standard mechanical Singer and an industrial-looking Serger with four threads, able to stitch up anything with a professional edge. Since learning how to sew from her mother-in-law fifty years prior, Mom became an excellent seamstress and sewed four of her daughters' wedding and bridesmaid dresses. For a couple years while living at The Village, Mom took in sewing alterations for fellow residents and seemed to enjoy both the work and the attention. She also showed her granddaughters, Haley and Maddie, around her machines but was too proficient to have much patience in teaching and demonstrating all their features. Haley still has the stuffed denim whale Maddie "made" for her with help from Mom. I was proud of Mom for keeping up this hobby and interest and taking the initiative to share her skills with others. Sewing and sharing her skills seemed to fill up her soul and was something for her—something she could be proud of, too.

When around other people, namely her peers at The Village, Mom became a different person I didn't recognize. She enjoyed getting dressed up but was frustrated in her later years with her limited options of clothes fitting her bony frame and that she could easily manage to put on by herself with her arthritic fingers. Dad used to buy her little diamond necklaces and earrings as gifts over the years, which frustrated her because she really preferred the trendy, more eye-catching pieces. In her later years, we girls helped her replace the clasps on these nicer items with the kind that closed with a magnet that she could more easily take on and off herself.

Once she invited me to The Village lounge with her for a glass of wine. She strutted in the door all gussied up with her sparkly pullover, black pants, colorful jewelry, and lipstick, holding her cane more like a prop from a Charlie Chaplin movie than a necessary mobility tool. I hung back and enjoyed the performance. The dark wood and burgundy carpet lounge was a staged scene from *The Shining* complete with smirking, jacket-clad barman, polishing glasses while listening to customer banter. "Hi, Jeff. How are you making your Chardonnay this evening?" Mom teased the bartender, easily fifty years her junior.

"Hey, Robert and John. What's happening tonight? Are you two being good?" she bantered, turning to two gray-haired jovial gentlemen sitting at a round table with their cocktails half gone. I shook my head and rolled my eyes in amazement. I had just watched my mother go from a griping, decrepit, female, seventy-five-year-old Scrooge to flirty teenager in six seconds flat. It had to have been a new world record.

I held on to those few brief moments when she seemed content in her surroundings. But it never lasted. Back in her apartment she'd continue to gripe and bitch about her doctor's shortcomings, her growing inabilities due to RA, why her other daughters didn't come visit or call her more often, how she couldn't sleep at night, and on and on and on. I have to think she tried to fit in those first few years at The Village—I see evidence of it now, so many years later. But her effect to those closest to her was of an unhappy woman, going it alone with everyone against her.

I believed for years Mom suffered from depression most of her life. I read, and even proposed to her doctor, that her long-term depression had led to a kind of dementia. In one study of 1,700 people average age of seventy-seven, investigators found high levels of depression prior to a diagnosis of dementia are linked to a more drastic decrease in thinking and memory skills later on (WebMD, 2014). Other such research poses the chicken or the egg scenario: "Does being diagnosed with dementia cause a senior to become depressed, or is late-life depression a precursor to future cognitive impairment?"

Mom's anger and bitterness grew over her years at The Village, and I found it confusing, troublesome, frustrating, and exhaustive. I assumed the years of living in pain and depression had made her this way, but I wanted to solve all her problems, make her happy. Surely, someone could do something about it, something could alter her life perspective for the better. Her health continued to be a growing issue, and I recognize in hindsight the irrecoverable downward spiral she was on.

One early afternoon, I stopped by Mom's apartment to simply say hello. I hadn't seen her in a couple weeks. At the front door of her apartment, I paused and took a deep breath. I needed to brace myself for entering back into her world, so different from mine, a world I worked so hard to keep at bay. Fido barked at me from the dark woods inside, calling me to come find him in his world of desperation, loneliness, unhappiness, anger, darkness. I got sucked in every time. The days I didn't have to think about being with her, I could free myself of the burden of her presence, her existence, my self-imposed responsibility for her happiness.

Standing at Mom's front door that day, I looked down at the brown, crispy bougainvillea plant Rhonda had sent her for Valentine's Day the past February. Mom loved receiving the beautiful vine, its flowers growing around the arched wire inside the pot. However, she couldn't care for it, almost as she lacked the ability to care for herself. I knocked on the door and turned the knob as I always did, but the door was uncharacteristically locked. Mom rarely locked her doors, apparently not afraid of (or without a care for) what other people could or would do to her or her belongings if they got in. I knocked again, starting to feel inside my purse for keys, and called, "Mom? It's me." A few seconds later she abruptly opened the door, a scowl on her face.

"Hi, Mom. How are you?" I asked suspiciously, wondering what had her so annoyed.

"I'm fine," she sighed, sitting at one end of the oval table just inside the door.

I sat down at the other end and asked again, "How are you? What's going on?"

"Nothing. Nothing is going on, as usual," she huffed. "Where have you been?" Her eyes seared into me.

"I've been busy, Mom." I said, feeling guilty I had no real excuse for my absence, or at least no excuse she would accept.

I began to tell her about my day and the news about her grandchildren, but she looked around distractedly, nervously, wringing her hands. She didn't appear to be listening. "I don't know what to do with this bill from the doctor's office," she interrupted, tossing me a paper from a pile of unopened mail in front of her. "My insurance should cover all this. They are crooks." Her bill involved a small amount and probably a co-pay; I wasn't concerned. "I'm not going to pay it," she barked.

"Hmm. Okay?" I responded, knowing I would take care of it. She and I had a joint account at the bank, and since she never looked at her statements, she would never question the debit.

"What's all this?" I asked her, reaching for the dozen or so items of unopened mail beneath her clasped hands.

"I don't know," she snapped, unconcerned, looking away toward the kitchen. I sifted through the pile, mostly junk, but pulled out a couple of Medicare and other insurance statements, some a few weeks old. I had kept a general watch over Mom's finances, but in the moment, I realized I should be more proactive. This understanding both irritated and exhausted me. The emotional and physical capacity to keep the Titanic of my and my mom's lives afloat exasperated me.

We sat in pained silence for a few moments with seemingly no common ground to connect on. Mom glanced up at me with a grimace and said with a furrowed brow, "What do you want?"

I shrugged, holding back the boiling rage building up inside me. "Mom, what do *you* want? What can I do to make *your* life better?" I said with more than a little sarcasm.

"Goodbye, Tracy," she huffed, sticking her chin out and pushing herself up off the chair. She turned her back to me and hobbled to her bedroom. Concentrating on staying composed, I gathered the mail and papers from the table into a folder. I couldn't reach her. I couldn't deal with her negativity, her naysaying, her absolute rejection of any type of suggestion, compliment, or conversation I posed. I paced into the kitchen to take a breath before leaving and found two empty wine bottles on the counter next to the sink.

I held back the tears as I hustled back to my car. Slamming the car door, I couldn't contain the internal fury any longer. I started screaming, releasing some tension of nearly fifty years trying to please her and everyone else outside of myself. Why does she make me so crazy? Why do I *let* her make me so crazy? Am I just trying to control her? I sobbed to myself. What makes a person hold fast to misery, disease, righteousness, closing themself off from help, support, love?

I called Colleen, a nurse at an assisted living facility in Wisconsin, who helped pull me back to sanity from my encounter. She doesn't remember, but she was my outlet during this time. She understood how difficult Mom could be and had the ability to offer an empathetic ear and reserved calm by being so far removed from day-to-day interaction with her.

When I reflect on this moment, I see this as a turning point in my awareness. I was never going to make Mom happy or content or fix all her problems. More importantly, maybe, I realized it wasn't my job. When Mom moved back into my life at close distance, I succumbed to my younger self's need to please her, be the peacekeeper, and make my outside world okay so I could somehow be all right. A door I left open for her to show me love and let me know I mattered closed gingerly and not without sorrow. At that time, I hadn't made the tiny realization that leaving the door open was futile and an impossible way to live. I wouldn't recognize this until a while after Mom's death.

These events that took place in my life then are compartmentalized. Will's OCD, Mom and Dad's physical decline, Mom in Gainesville, two teenage daughters, soccer mom duties, and work responsibilities were all separated in my mind as detached and insular periods. But years later when I look back, these things all happened concurrently within a six-year period, and both Bryce and I are incredulous at how we managed to survive, our marriage as well as our sanity.

Somewhere inside me I found empathy for myself I had, before then, labeled as selfishness. A line had been crossed in my mind. Mom wasn't going to be the person I wanted her to be or knew she could be, for whatever reason, and I couldn't change that. I had a lot going on in my life, people who counted on me, but from this time period on I knew I had to take care of myself. As I did with my depression and Will's OCD and some of Mom's health issues, I sought support and understanding in books and research. I devoured the latest in personal growth and leadership, psychology, neuroscience, and spirituality that continues today.

DECLINE

———

"Death is the enemy. But the enemy has superior forces. Eventually, it wins. And in a war that you cannot win, you don't want a general who fights to the point of total annihilation. You don't want Custer. You want Robert E. Lee, someone who knows how to fight for territory that can be won and how to surrender it when it can't, someone who understands that the damage is greatest if all you do is battle to the bitter end."
—ATUL GAWANDE, *BEING MORTAL*

Mom was not well, physically or mentally. No matter how much I wanted to believe she could recover, change, or feel better, it just wasn't going to happen. No matter how many times I expected it to be different it wasn't. Each time the dance was the same, but I expected a different outcome, a different partner. I put my hand in the fire and expected it not to burn. I wanted that soccer mom who piled the team in the car before a big game, that perfect TV parent who oversaw the well-being of her children with an assured smile, that engaged mom who pointed out puppy dogs to us in the puffy clouds while lying in the cool grass on warm summer afternoons.

By the time she got to Gainesville, Mom was too ill, too lost, too rigid in her beliefs. I had begun to forgive her for what I thought she should or shouldn't be doing for herself or me. I had put some distance between her destiny and my ability to direct it. I resigned myself to an emotionless and reserved relationship that wasn't going to change no matter how much I wanted and needed her to show me she cared. I had given what I knew to give her, to the relationship, but never got anything back. That could be the tragedy of this story, but the meat of it really is I was only able to give her as much as I knew to give. She taught me her version of love, her version of how to live a life, and I emulated that version back to her and to the world.

Mom's last several years on this planet were fraught with pain and suffering. She wouldn't let me or anyone comfort her. Bitterness embodied her essence. She didn't seem to want anything different or to give life anything more. She seemed to be waiting for life to give her something, validate her in some way. It didn't and never could.

She took myriad prescriptions and over the counter medications for decades to help her manage the pain of rheumatoid arthritis (RA). In her early fifties she had her first of three bilateral hip replacements due to degenerative osteoarthritis. In her later years, doctors treated her for ovarian and colon cancer, abdominal adhesions, bent fingers, cellulitis, and more. She had continual health issues needing treatment. Her health and care organized her days as it does many an elder person. Pill bottles took a glorified, worshipped position on nightstands, kitchen counters, and bathroom cabinets. Looking back now, I think, *How could anyone not have compassion and empathy for someone in this position?* I did have compassion. It just bounced off an impenetrable brick wall.

The last year she and Dad visited Florida over winter, two years before he died, I remember the kids' and my final visit to their rental two hours west in Hernando Beach. Mom walked around with a scowl, grimacing as she hobbled about in a lot of pain. Dad seemed more forgetful than ever—a side effect from the dose of brain radiation he had after his cancer discovery eight years earlier. Add on his deteriorating hearing—he'd grumble when asked to use his hearing aid—and it wasn't the best visit. Dad enjoyed the kids, as he always did. They seemed to annoy Mom at some level, but they could always make her smile.

The Saturday evening following the visit, I got a call from Dad saying he had taken Mom to the nearest hospital about twenty minutes away in Spring Hill. In that moment I was more concerned he had driven. He drove precariously, and we all knew it, even him. He said Mom had been complaining about hip pain since she stepped off the exercise bicycle the day before.

"What was she doing on the exercise bicycle?" I asked in disbelief. She already seemed in so much pain I couldn't imagine why she would get on the unfamiliar contraption.

"I don't know," he replied, a little confused.

I dropped everything and headed to Hernando Beach to see how I could help. But, of course, with Mom nobody could help. She had decided the hospital—a small, rural acute care facility—was inept at caring for patients. "I waited *two* hours in the waiting room before they even looked at me!" she complained. "They just shook their heads when I asked them where the doctor was. Then I had to wait another hour for the x-ray to come back." The test came back negative for fracture or anything wrong. They gave her a prescription for her pain and sent her on her way.

Mom and Dad decided to head back to Iowa a few weeks early, and I helped them pack up. Neither fit to drive the twenty-three hours back home, Bryce took one for the team and drove the pair for the two-day journey. Bryce's jovial manner and colorful view of the world lent itself well to keeping the trip light and tolerable. Afterword, he only complained about one thing: his error in judgement in stopping overnight in one of Tennessee's nine dry counties. They all could've used a cocktail that night.

Upon returning to Iowa, an MRI revealed a hip fracture, and Mom was told to use a wheelchair and walker for the next several weeks to let it heal. Oh, and to quit smoking during the recovery.

Mom never quit smoking, and her hip continued to give her problems while she lived in Gainesville. At some point the replacement in her hip failed, and I took her to Orlando—a two-hour drive from Gainesville—to see a specialist to "redo" the surgery in what's called a revision total hip replacement. Mom sat on the exam table in the stark white room while the surgeon explained the procedure. "Okay. So, when can we get this thing scheduled?" Mom asked tersely.

"Well, first, I need you to know that you must stop smoking, or it won't last, and I won't agree to do the procedure," the surgeon explained, looking at Mom, then at me, then back at Mom.

I remember thinking, *Don't look at me! I am just the driver here.*

"Of course," Mom replied as she closed her eyes and jutted her chin up in the air.

After the procedure the surgeon came out to tell me it went well. He reiterated his instruction for her to stop smoking, at least for a few weeks while it healed. She didn't and was back on his table six months later for him to put screws in the hip to hold her crumbling bones together.

Mom was just generally not the ideal patient. Due to her couple of earlier abdominal surgeries, she developed adhesions, bands of scar-like tissue between two organs or tissues. One spring, she spent a week in the hospital each month for three months in a row for this condition.

By her third admission, I had researched alternative treatments for resolving them. One—specialized, deep tissue massage therapy—sounded promising. Standing at the foot of Mom's bed, I perked up when the admitting physician finally hustled into the room. Clipboard by his side, he flatly asked Mom, "How are you this morning?"

"How do you think I'm doing? I want to get out of here!" Mom barked.

"Well, you're here until you have a bowel movement, and then we'll see," he said with a slight upturn of his mouth. He was just as surly as she was.

"I did some research, and I think massage therapy might help these adhesions go away. What do you think?" I asked hopefully.

"Those sorts of alternative treatments never work, and you'll just end up spending time and money chasing them. You'll just have to get used to it. This is her life from here on out," he dismissed, and my jaw dropped. Did I detect some pleasure in his manner? This guy didn't seem to want his patient to get better. His name was Dr. Dick—no joke—and he lived up to the family legacy. I spoke to my neighbor who happened to be a physical therapist. She performed this procedure on Mom who received relief after a few sessions and never suffered in the hospital with this condition again.

I knew Mom experienced a lot of physical pain, and I had empathy for her. But her disagreeable temperament made it difficult for me to comfort and console her or just be there for her in her condition. She must have been lonely. She played blackjack on her electronic handheld game, continued to be an avid reader, and enjoyed solitaire on the computer when she could sit in the chair long enough. It became more and more frequent for Bryce or me to find her isolated in her apartment in the middle of the day, blinds closed and lights off, in bed taking a nap or playing her game. We hired a companion for her to come in two to three times per week to keep her company and go to the grocery store for her on occasion.

She drank her wine of choice, Chardonnay, more and more and ate less and less. During a period after a surgery when she couldn't drive, I picked up groceries for her which included a couple bottles of wine. When those were gone after a day and a half, and I refused to bring her another couple, she enlisted her friend Margie to go pick them up for her.

She eventually stopped sewing for other residents, and about a year before she died, I noticed she wasn't even reading anything anymore. I would swap murder mysteries between her and my father-in-law, but she eventually just lost interest. This was a huge red flag to me as she always had a book in her hand. I'm still not sure if she just didn't find them interesting anymore or if she experienced more of a cognitive decline than we knew. I suspected the latter. She would come over to our house for a visit but would inexplicably just get up and leave after about twenty minutes, saying she just needed to go home.

Mom's world kept getting smaller and smaller. Eventually it seemed to consist of worrying about medications and drinking wine to pass the time. She had limited herself to driving only to Publix Super Market about a mile up the road, so I picked up anything else she needed that she couldn't get there. She wanted some dresses she could pull over her head easily with no buttons or zippers—she couldn't navigate them with her arthritic hands, and they might scratch her paper-thin skin. So, I made a mall run, grabbed a dozen or so dresses her size, and took them back to her for approval. She maybe kept one or two, and looked at the rest with disdain, not even trying them on. She wanted something colorful, and it wasn't easy in our college town to find garments with a length at or below the knee to fit her other requirements.

One morning as I got ready for work, she called me on my phone. "Tracy! Tracy! Help! I've fallen. It hurts! It hurts!"

"Call 9-1-1," I directed. "I'll be right there." When I got to her apartment, a staff person from The Village was there, and I found Mom lying down next to her bed sobbing in pain. She had once again fractured her hip. Because of her physical condition, surgery was not an option to aid in the healing. Instead, she was admitted to a skilled nursing and rehabilitation facility to recover.

In rehab, Mom became a chained, rabid dog, lashing out at everyone and anyone who came in to assist her. She refused the prescribed physical and occupational therapy. When her doctor came in to check on her and coax her into complying with therapy orders, she just yelled at him, "Just get me out of here. I want to go home. I just want to go home!"

On the advice of my sister, Colleen, I spoke with Mom's doctor separately about options for putting Mom under hospice care. I learned hospice care is not only for terminal cancer patients but can provide pain management and support for patients at end of life for a number of chronic illnesses. Mom's recurrent falls, fractures, and significant weight loss seemed to support her eligibility, but her doctor didn't agree. He also said if she refused to agree to therapy, she would be discharged from rehab, and we all knew she couldn't manage living by herself in her apartment.

I don't remember moving Mom's things into the assisted living facility (ALF) that summer. Everything is a blur. She couldn't afford this service at The Village, so we opted to move her to a stand-alone ALF on the southwest side of town. There she would receive help bathing and dressing, getting in and out of bed and into her wheelchair, medication management, and more. Mom resisted, but she had no choice. It was the middle of the month, so we were able to keep her apartment at The Village and take a few more weeks to completely pack up her things.

While we transitioned her medical authorization and prescriptions to the new ALF, I had to manage her pain medication. I brought medications to the nurse at the facility and signed off on pill numbers and dosage. A few days in, the nurse informed me this was taken care of, and the ALF would now receive and dispense them to her. However, on the first Saturday afternoon Mom was there, she called me saying her prescription had run out, and she was in pain. The nurse told me I would have to get a new one until the pills showed up at the facility. I panicked.

I took Mom's call standing on the sidelines of my son's soccer game. My hands shook as I walked over to beneath some bleachers, in the shade and out of earshot of other parents, to make some phone calls. I got Mom's doctor's answering service, and I paced, taking deep calming breaths, while waiting for the return phone call.

"Well, we are dealing with opioids, here. It's unlikely we can get her another prescription without an in-person visit," the doctor said matter-of-factly. "I'll call her physician directly and see what he says."

I started breathing fast and deep. It was Saturday. My mom was in pain. She wouldn't last until Monday without something to help her. I filed through all possible ideas in my head: Did we have any leftover pain meds at home from a previous dental surgery? Do I know anyone who has recently had surgery? I wonder how many Advil it would take to control the pain without overdosing her? Do I know anyone who could get me some pills from the street? No part of me wanted my mother to suffer, but the world of managing her healthcare and her overall abominable disposition was like slowly walking barefoot on hot coals. And it was my choice. I didn't have to respond. I didn't have to care. I could have ignored Mom's phone calls. I could have waited until Monday to call her doctor for more pills or let her wait until the ALF got the prescription. I could have hung up the phone and sat back down on my chair on the sidelines with the other soccer moms. But I couldn't do that. I needed to help her get some relief, and although I'm not proud of it, in the back of my mind I just wanted her to go away and leave me alone.

I hustled to Publix, the moseying Saturday shoppers around me falling to the background as I pressed my chest into the high counter at the pharmacy window. It was a dream scene from a movie, the surrounding setting blurred with just a circle framed around me in focus. Nothing else mattered at that moment. My hand shook as I gave the printed oxycodone prescription I managed to get from Mom's doctor through the window to the young technician. I could feel my chest pounding. The technician looked at the prescription then up at me suspiciously. She asked Mom's birth date and address, typed a few things into her computer, looked at me, looked back at the prescription and said, "It looks like this was just filled a few days ago. I can't fill any more until Monday."

"No, no, no, no," I pleaded, shaking my head. I told her my story, my eyes filling with tears, voice shaky. She probably saw me as an addict, trembling from withdrawal. She got the pharmacist involved who made some calls and was able to get it filled. In my head I had already decided to try Walgreens, Walmart, and the independent pharmacy down the road I couldn't remember the name of. I was going to get the prescription filled somewhere.

I brought Mom her meds, saw her swallow the pills, and tucked her in bed. I called her the next morning, and she said she was fine and sounded good. Feeling uneasy she had enough pain pills to last her a few more days, I visited her later that day. It was early evening, and I found Mom's dinner on a tray on her dresser. "Did you eat any dinner? Are you hungry?" I commented.

"I had a bite, but it's not very good," she replied, pulling her legs onto the bed and struggling to get the covers over them. She had always gone to bed early, and I didn't find it too odd her turning out the light so early. I helped her with her blanket, patted her arm, and told her good night while turning off her bed lamp.

Still feeling unsettled about how she was doing, I stopped by to check on her on my way to work the next morning. At seven thirty in the morning, I found Mom dressed in one of the flowery dresses I bought her, slumped in her wheelchair in the middle of the common room and drooling as she weakly cried, "Help me. Help me." I looked around and saw a scene from *One Flew Over the Cuckoo's Nest*, one nurse behind a counter and plexiglass wall counting pills, another shuffling papers in her office, door open and in view, and a resident staring at us blankly from her own wheelchair across the room.

"Mom, Mom! Are you okay?" I asked.

"I have to go to the bathroom," she muttered. Looking around the room again, I grabbed the handles on the back of her wheelchair and hustled her to her room. Somehow I managed to wrangle my arms around her ninety-five-pound frame and half-lifted, half-dragged her into the bathroom and onto the toilet. She was still slumped over as I held her steady on the stool. She was trying to say something, but her speech was slurred. She swayed to and fro. Not seeing how I could manage to get a good enough grip on her to get her out of the bathroom and back into her wheelchair, I hit the nurse call button on wall. No response. I hit it again. No response. With one arm around Mom's shoulders, I reached over and inside my purse for my cell phone and dialed 9-1-1.

The hospital doctors diagnosed Mom with sepsis as a result of acute bacterial pneumonia. Waiting in the emergency room bay for a hospital bed, Mom floated in and out of consciousness. The staff asked me some questions about her health history and if she smoked and how much. "Probably about a pack a day at least," I answered.

Mom stirred angrily and said something unintelligible while shaking her head, eyes still closed. I smile at the memory today: I always nagged her to quit smoking, and she always grumbled back at me about it. Even in her subconscious state, it was a constant in our relationship.

After finally settling Mom in her hospital room that night, I held her hand as she lay unconscious and motionless in the bed. She was in an awkward position—head tilted up and angled forward, arms at her sides but apart from her body, and knees bent to the side. I put a pillow underneath her knees, attempting to adjust them like I knew she preferred. I stroked her gray hair away from her forehead, a strange intimacy I couldn't imagine doing when she was awake. Before I left, I kissed her forehead and told her I would be back in the morning to check on her. The thought crossed my mind that she might die overnight, but I had thought that before and she always managed to surprise me and rally back. She was tough, both inside and out.

I was alone when I got the news of Mom's death early the next morning. My husband and kids were two states away on a church mission trip. I hung up the phone and sat propped up in bed, my back on the headboard and knees bent under the sheet, the nightstand light still on. All I heard was the quiet in the room, in my head. I didn't cry. I didn't think. I was numb. It was over. I hoped Mom was finally at peace, finally subdued. I hoped she finally found whatever she was looking for.

EPILOGUE

———

"None of us can undo what we've done, or relive a life already recorded."

—MITCH ALBOM, *TUESDAYS WITH MORRIE*

When I take a deep breath, it feels selfish. It feels really good and cleansing, but it still feels really selfish. It's something for me, something I need. But, somehow, something to be ashamed of. Somewhere I learned or was conditioned to believe that what I needed didn't matter. That I was less than other people in the room. I took on my parents' baggage but now know it was never mine to carry. I don't blame my mother. I don't blame my parents or the way they raised me. Compared to many people, my youth and upbringing were magical, glorious experiences, and I am not complaining.

As much as I share in the previous pages my struggle with my mother and how crazy she made me feel as an adult, Mom taught me many things I'm grateful for. Mom demonstrated strength and independence, and I see and value those qualities within myself. I can hold firm to my convictions and am steadfast in them until proven otherwise. My mother, although a high school dropout, was a seeker and learner through most of her adult life. Before her youngest daughter died, she read widely about astronomy, astrology, and religion and shared her learnings with her young daughters. Once diagnosed with rheumatoid arthritis she researched natural health and homeopathic remedies to support her body's immune system, mailing me the books, recipes, and newsletters she received when done. This taught me to do my own research and find answers to questions myself, pivotal when seeking information and support for depression, OCD, and abdominal adhesions, among other things.

I recognize a resilience in myself I can only attribute to my mother. It's like a steel rod inside me from my head to my lower sternum, unmovable and rigid, that defines me. I embrace this strength but also acknowledge it can come across as cold and inflexible, I can hide behind it when my feelings and softness start to come to the surface. I am learning, as I embrace my strength, to give space for the feelings to show up, come up for air, breathe. I recognize that to do so, *that* is how to live. *That* is what it means to live fully. Only then can we show up as fully baked humans, able to make and sustain connections with each other. All these things I've realized were part of my experience of childhood emotional neglect, all adult manifestations of it. Discovering this, recognizing this, has been a game changer for me.

Recently, I read two memoirs with passages that stood out to me as I wrote this book. In *I Am Not What I Am,* author Tom Linde, a clinical psychologist with severe cerebral palsy, wrote about how his parents approached his physical limitations: "You need to find other ways of getting around, and work to train the parts of your brain that were not injured to work extra hard to give you better control of your speech and hands." Good, pragmatic advice that served him for getting around in the world. But Linde notes this advice, "… helped me gloss over a bundle of unresolved matters for many years. It did not allow for the caring exploration of feeling."

Advice for Linde to focus on doing, on acting, on navigating the practical resonates with me. I, too, received all sorts of advice for living in the world but no guidance on managing or acknowledging the feelings inherent to myself, innate to all of us as human beings. This acknowledgement, I've learned, is crucial to developing oneself as a whole person, able to fully live and thrive in a chaotic, unpredictable, sometimes disturbing world.

Lucy Grealy in her memoir, *Autobiography of a Face*, shares her revelation that she is more than her face. At age nine, she was disfigured after surgery and radiation for a type of bone cancer and multiple attempts to reconstruct it:

"Without another operation to hang all my hopes on, I was completely on my own. And now something inside me started to miss me. A part of me, one that had always been there, organically knew I was whole. It was as if this part had known it was necessary to wait so long, to wait until the impatient din around it had quieted down until the other internal voices had grown exhausted and hoarse before it could begin to speak, before I would begin to listen."

The internal voice in my head was silenced a bit that day in my car after visiting my mother. I finally acknowledged what I was resisting was me. Not able to change my external world, all I had was me. I could control me. So, I began listening to myself and what I could actually control and change. I began a lone journey to find myself again—I had run away from myself and longed to come back.

In Brené Brown's book *Dare to Lead*, she presents the idea that "people are doing the best that they can" in any moment and how remembering this can lead to empathy for others and their situation. She writes:

"One woman said, 'If this was true and my mother was doing the best she can, I would be grief-stricken. I'd rather be angry than sad, so it's easier to believe she's letting me down on purpose than to grieve the fact that my mother is never going to be who I need her to be.'"

This was me. For some reason I resisted having empathy for my mom. I'd rather blame her for what she didn't give me than think about how she grew up and what she did or didn't receive throughout her childhood and life. That's what this book has given me—the opportunity to reflect on all that and forgive her—and myself—for being human and needing love.

Three years after Mom died, Bryce and I took some friends to the Iowa State Fair. While there, we stopped briefly at my childhood friend Laurie's house. I had confided in Laurie about my relationship with my mom before she died and how frustrated I was. Before we left, Laurie pulled me aside and asked, "Did you get things resolved with your mom before she passed?"

That was a great question. I answered truthfully, "Yes. It wasn't perfect, but I'm at peace with it, with her."

I've written this book in the context of CEN, reflecting on my life with that in mind to understand and make sense of my relationship with my mother. However, we had plenty of good times, and I don't want to come across as crass or uncaring. I could easily write another book only looking at the good times, and it would be completely different but equally true. The question is: How do we want to look back on our lives? Do we want to remember and dwell on just the bad parts? We can, but we can just as easily remember the good times. It's our choice.

Eckhart Tolle in his book, *The Power of Now*, extols the virtue of forgetting the past as the past. It serves no purpose to dwell on what happened yesterday or even one minute ago. I agree, but for me great value and healing has come from exploring my relationship with my mother. I also appreciate the value of sharing one's story as a way of connecting to one another's common human condition.

I can take the strength Mom gave me and embrace it but not let it overpower me. I don't have to be the woman my mother demonstrated to me. I don't have to reject all of her. I can take what she gave me and manifest it in the world as a gift for myself as well as for others. I don't have to be ashamed of this realization. That is what life is for—to learn, to grow from our experiences and from the past that's been given to us and that we've had a hand in creating, consciously or not.

Sometimes when I lie on my stomach in bed at night, I think of Mom. It feels good for a while, healing. Somehow when I do, Mom is there, too. Maybe it's the whole front half of my body touching and being coddled by the mattress bringing the essence of what I needed from Mom and never got. Nonetheless, I am comforted and healed from the inside out.

ACKNOWLEDGEMENTS

———

I have wanted to write this book for years, even prior to Mom moving near me and passing away. It has been inside me for a long time. It never would have been written without a series of events that started with writing down what I wanted to do in my life as a "bucket list." Writing it down is one thing, but saying it out loud and actually doing it are completely different beasts. That is where these acknowledgements must start.

During a session with Taylor Williams (my "Covid Coach") I admitted, "I want to write this book that's inside me but I'm not writing. I don't know what to do." She helped me think through what was blocking me and a few weeks later shared that she was writing a book through a great program and that I should check it out. I called Eric Koester, the founder and CEO of Book Creators at Creator Institute, and dove in. Thank you, Taylor, for opening the door and Eric for welcoming me into this process to become an author.

The built-in support and accountability system at Book Creators and New Degree Press was the only way I would have made it through this process. Thank you to my editors, Katie Sigler, Mary Ann Tate, Carol McKibben, and Amanda

Brown, for your invaluable feedback, unending patience and priceless insights.

Immense thanks go to my Beta readers for their patience and diligence in giving me feedback prior to publishing: Colleen Barber, Celia Burger, Donna McCart-Welser, Michele Rogers, and Dorene Webster.

I appreciate those who took time to remember with me and share their viewpoint of our common history together: my Aunt Evie and Aunt Cathey, my Uncle John, my children Haley, Madison, and Will, and my sisters Colleen, Rhonda, Jill, and Kelly. Thank you to Dr. Joe McNamara for being a valuable resource and helping me think through how to frame the obsessive-compulsive disorder discussion.

Thank you to my early supporters who pre-ordered the book and made publication possible: Tania Alavi, Melissa Alton, Adam and Rachel Alty, Clare Anderson, Steve Anderson, Greg and Colleen Barber, Sue Bellmer, Sue Berg, Rae Berggren, Laurie Bianchi, Carissa Blaser, Donna Boatman, Trish Bohr, Janet and EJ Bolduc, Andy Bradfield, Gail Brill, Cynthia Brown, Lisa Brown, Makayla Buchanan, Bill and Donna Buhi, Amy Burger, Ben and Susan Burger, Bryce Burger, Bill and Celia Burger, Maddie Burger, Matt Burger, Sarah Burger, Will Burger, David and Linda Busch, Ross and Haley Busch, Dawn Byrne, Cindy Caldwell, Jason Castillo, Lisa Chacon, Mary Chance, Chris Clore, Marcey Corey, Mary Lou Crawford, Rosemary and Francis Davis, Teresa Dejohn, Beth Deluzain, Kathy Dixon, Steve and Peggy Emerson, Jennifer Ethridge, Cynthia Falardeau, Pam Fehlhafer, Dave Ferro, Tommy and Dana Fillmer, Catherine Fluck-Price, Sartaj Gill, Aimee Green, Katie Gunter, Annastacia Hackett, Carol Hackett, Stephanie Hackett, Beth Haines, Missy Hanssen, Kathy

Harris, Jamie Harter, Tara Hatfield, Desiree Hayes, Jamar Hebert, Kathy Herndon, Kim Higgins, Mary Louise Hildreth, Joe and Kelly Hintzen, Becker Holland, John Hopkins, Gwen Howard, Priscilla Howard, Teresa Howell, Linda Hudson, Lynn Hughes, Brian Hurley, Cathy Ipser, Theresa Jenkins, Dan and Jan Johnson, Greg Johnson, Dug Jones, Kim Jowell, Jack Kindschuh, Amy Kirby, Dave and Peggy Kochert, Anne Koon, Kristin Kozelsky, Mary Lane, Cathy Locklear, Jeannette MacFadden, Margaret Madden, Ally Magnee Madden, Larry Marshall, Laure Martin, Mary Marx, Donna McCart-Welser, Carol McKibbin, Lisa Meline, Justin Michalman, Toby Monaco, James Morris, Leza Mueller, Shirley Newson, Lorie Noe, Todd and Kathy Olson, Ed Osborne, Jane Page, Amy Pearson, Betsy Pepine, Cathey Petersen, Anthony Pierce, Scott Pifer, Susan Pilon, Jill Pompeu, Steve Price, Connie Quincey, Carol Ramirez, Cynthia Ramirez, Chris Riggs, Missy Robinson, Rich and Michelle Ropp, David Rountree, Laurie Schafer, Kathy Schofield, Andrew Seim, Cynthia Shelamer, Linda Singleton, Kathie Southwick, Roger Stroud, Jennifer Tam, Joe and Claudia Templeton, Kelly Thawley, Tori Thiessen, Pat Thomas, Teddy Thompson, Donna Jo Toney, Lyn Von Sprecken, Kellie Weber, Dorene Webster, Matt and Anita Webster, Mary Ann Williams, Taylor Williams, Amy Wilson, Lisa Wilson, Mary K Wimsett, Carol Winborn, Evie and John Wright, Martha Wright, Brooklyn Young, and Carole Zegel.

To my husband, Bryce: thank you for helping me make sense of this life. You've shared most of it with me, like it or not. You didn't know what you were getting into, and I love you for sticking in here with me.

The cover photograph is of the pastel *Girl on a Swing* by Joan Mulgrew. Thank you Sam Mulgrew and the Mulgrew family for permission to utilize this beautiful piece of work created by your late mother.

Thank you to Pace Center for Girls, Inc. for supporting this project. Pace is a national organization that envisions a world where all girls and young women have power, in a just and equitable society. Founded in 1985, Pace provides free year-round middle and high school academics, case management, counseling, and life skills development in a safe and supportive environment. Pace schools recognize and deal with each student's past trauma and build upon girl's individual strengths. Dedicated to meeting the social, emotional, and educational needs of girls, Pace has a successful and proven program model that has changed the life trajectory of more than forty thousand girls. It is recognized as one of the nation's leading advocates for girls in need. For more information on Pace Center for Girls, visit www.pacecenter. org. Part of the proceeds from my book sales are going to the Pace Center in Alachua, Florida.

APPENDIX

———

AUTHOR'S NOTE

Lamott, Anne. *Bird by Bird: Some Instructions on Writing and Life.* New York: Anchor Books, 1995.

Rogers, Michele. *The Wounding and Healing of the Mother-Daughter Relationship.* (Master's thesis, Pacifica Graduate Institute, 2010). https://www.proquest.com/docview/276242957?pq-origsite=gscholar&fromopenview=true.

Webb, Jonice. *Running on Empty: Overcome Your Childhood Emotional Neglect.* New York: Morgan James Publishing, 2014.

THE GREEN HOUSE

Hayes, Stephen C. *A Liberated Mind: How to Pivot Toward What Matters.* New York: Avery, 2020.

DICK AND MARY

Heller, Diane Poole. *Healing Your Attachment Wounds: How to Create Deep and Lasting Intimate Relationships.* Read by Diane Poole Heller. Louisville: Sounds True, 2017. Audiobook audio ed., 6 hr., 6 min.

DAISY

Roll, Rich. *Finding Ultra: Rejecting Middle Age, Becoming One of the World's Fittest Men, and Discovering Myself.* New York: Three Rivers Press, 2013.

Stoneson, Ann. "What Makes a People Pleaser." *Labyrinth Healing,* May 8, 2022. https://labyrinthhealing.com/blog/what-makes-a-people-pleaser.

EAST SHAULIS ROAD

Hayes, Stephen C. *A Liberated Mind: How to Pivot Toward What Matters.* New York: Avery, 2020.

Oommen, Anita M. *Picking Up the Shards: Healing the Pain of Mother-Wounds, Discovering the Mother-Heart of God.* Dallas: Oxborough, 2019.

Webb, Jonice. "Why Emotional Neglect and Depression Are Often Experienced Together." *Finding Meaning Articles,* October 17, 2018. https://drjonicewebb.com/why-emotional-neglect-and-depression-are-often-experienced-together/?fbclid=IwAR3hzY8b9LtxeYdQCyGo-A3ErT2Rz8-blOmnzGljM-FouyT9jouEkSIgBxks.

JENNY

Chris, Grace, George Bonanno, Ruth Malkinson, and Simon Rubin. "Appendix E: Bereavement Experiences After the Death of a Child." In *When Children Die: Improving Palliative and End-of-Life Care for Children and Their Families.* Institute of Medicine (US) Committee on Palliative and End-of-Life Care for Children and Their Families, edited by M.J. Field and R.E. Behrman. Washington D.C.: National Academies Press, 2003.

Kessler, David. *Finding Meaning: The Sixth Stage of Grief.* New York: Scribner, 2019.

IGUANA

Minot, Susan. "Forty Portraits in Forty Years." *The New York Times Magazine,* October 3, 2014. https://www.nytimes.com/interactive/2014/10/03/magazine/01-brown-sisters-forty-years.html.

Tannen, Deborah. *You Were Always Mom's Favorite!: Sisters in Conversation Throughout Their Lives.* New York: Ballentine Books, 2010.

ADRIFT

Atwood, Margaret. *The Handmaid's Tale.* New York: Anchor Books, 1998.

Hart Research Associates. *Falling Short? College Learning and Career Success: Selected Findings from Online Surveys of Employers and College Students Conducted on Behalf of the Association of American Colleges and Universities.* Washington, D.C.: Hart Research Associates, 2015. https://dgmg81phhvh63.

cloudfront.net/content/user-photos/Research/PDFs/2015em-
ployerstudentsurvey.pdf.

Pulmer, Brad. "Only 27 Percent of College Grads Have a Job Related
to Their Major." *The Washington Post,* May 20, 2013. https://
www.washingtonpost.com/news/wonk/wp/2013/05/20/only-
27-percent-of-college-grads-have-a-job-related-to-their-major/.

Webb, Jonice. "Why Emotional Neglect and Depression Are Often
Experienced Together." *Finding Meaning Articles,* October 17,
2018. https://drjonicewebb.com/why-emotional-neglect-and-de-
pression-are-often-experienced-together/?fbclid=IwAR3hzY-
8b9LtxeYdQCyGo-A3ErT2Rz8-blOmnzGljMFouyT9jouEkSIg-
Bxks.

THE BLACK DOG

ABC News. "PrimeTime: Carrie Fisher Interview." *Shows.* December
21, 2000. https://abcnews.go.com/Primetime/story?id=132315.

Burns, David D. *Feeling Good: The New Mood Therapy.* New York:
Avon Books, 1980.

Quotefancy. *Cindy Crawford Quotes.* Accessed May 21, 2022. https://
quotefancy.com/cindy-crawford-quotes.

NUMBNESS

Beck, Martha. *The Way of Integrity: Finding the Path to Your True
Self.* New York: An Open Field, 2021.

MONSOON SEASON BEGINS

Campbell, Joseph. *The Hero with a Thousand Faces (The Collected Works of Joseph Campbell)*. Novato: New World Library, 2008.

International OCD Foundation. "Who Gets OCD?" *For Kids,* Accessed February 9, 2022. https://kids.iocdf.org/what-is-ocd-kids/who-gets-ocd/.

Khouri, Callie, dir. *Divine Secrets of the Ya-Ya Sisterhood.* 2002; Burbank, CA: Warner Brothers Pictures. DVD.

Lamott, Anne. *Dusk, Night, Dawn.* New York: Riverhead Books, 2021.

MOM IN GAINESVILLE

Carlson, Kathie. *In Her image: The Unhealed Daughter's Search for Her Mother.* Boulder: Shambhala Publications, 1989.

Singer, Michael. *The Untethered Soul: The Journey Beyond Yourself.* Oakland: New Harbinger Publications, 2007.

WebMD. "Light Shed on Link Between Depression, Dementia." *News.* July 30, 2014. https://www.webmd.com/depression/news/20140730/scientists-shed-light-on-link-between-depression-dementia.

DECLINE

Gawande, Atul. *Being Moral: Illness, Medicine and What Matters in the End.* New York: Picador, 2015.

EPILOGUE

Albom, Mitch. *Tuesdays with Morrie: An Old Man, a Young Man, and Life's Greatest Lesson.* New York: Broadway Books, 2002.

Brown, Brené. *Dare to Lead: Brave Work. Tough Conversations. Whole Hearts.* New York: Random House, 2018.

Grealy, Lucy. *Autobiography of a Face.* Boston: Mariner Books, 2016.

Linde, Thomas. *I Am Not What I Am: A Psychologist's Memoir. Notes on Managing Personal Misfortune.* Bloomington: Authorhouse, 2001.

Tolle, Eckhart. *The Power of Now: A Guide to Spiritual Enlightenment.* Novato: New World Library, 2004.